Independence Educational Publishers

First published by Independence Educational Publishers

The Studio, High Green

Great Shelford

Cambridge CB22 5EG

England

© Independence 2018

Copyright

Photocopy licence

ISBN-13: 978 1 86168 788 3

Printed in Great Britain

Zenith Print Group

Contents

Introduction

FACTS ABOUT SMOKING is Volume 337 in the **ISSUES** series. The aim of the series is to offer current, diverse information about important issues in our world, from a UK perspective.

ABOUT FACTS ABOUT SMOKING

Smoking is the biggest cause of preventable deaths in England, accounting for more than 80,000 deaths each year. One in two smokers will die from a smoking-related disease. This book explores the many health issues faced by smokers, from heart problems to cancer. It looks at the possible damage done to people exposed to second-hand smoke. It also explores what effect the smoking ban has had and if it has helped to reduce the numbers of people who smoke.

OUR SOURCES

Titles in the **ISSUES** series are designed to function as educational resource books, providing a balanced overview of a specific subject.

The information in our books is comprised of facts, articles and opinions from many different sources, including:

⇨ Newspaper reports and opinion pieces

⇨ Website factsheets

⇨ Magazine and journal articles

⇨ Statistics and surveys

⇨ Government reports

⇨ Literature from special interest groups.

A NOTE ON CRITICAL EVALUATION

Because the information reprinted here is from a number of different sources, readers should bear in mind the origin of the text and whether the source is likely to have a particular bias when presenting information (or when conducting their research). It is hoped that, as you read about the many aspects of the issues explored in this book, you will critically evaluate the information presented.

It is important that you decide whether you are being presented with facts or opinions. Does the writer give a biased or unbiased report? If an opinion is being expressed, do you agree with the writer? Is there potential bias to the 'facts' or statistics behind an article?

ASSIGNMENTS

In the back of this book, you will find a selection of assignments designed to help you engage with the articles you have been reading and to explore your own opinions. Some tasks will take longer than others and there is a mixture of design, writing and research-based activities that you can complete alone or in a group.

Useful weblinks

www.ashwales.org.uk

www.assets.publishing.service.gov.uk

www.bhf.org.uk

www.bristol.ac.uk

www.bupa.co.uk

www.theconversation.com

www.gateshead.gov.uk

www.gov.uk

www.huffingtonpost.co.uk

www.independent.co.uk

www.ncbi.nlm.nih.gov

www.nhs.uk

www.telegraph.co.uk

www.theguardian.com

www.who.int

FURTHER RESEARCH

At the end of each article we have listed its source and a website that you can visit if you would like to conduct your own research. Please remember to critically evaluate any sources that you consult and consider whether the information you are viewing is accurate and unbiased.

Effects of smoking

Smoking is the most common cause of death and disease that's entirely preventable. In the UK, more than 86,000 people die each year from smoking-related diseases. This equates to about half of all regular smokers dying because of their addiction.

Here we give you the facts about the harm smoking does to your body and advice on how to quit.

Why smoking is bad for you

Cancers

Smoking is by far the greatest avoidable risk for developing many types of cancer. These include cancer of your throat and mouth, and cancer of organs such as your lungs, stomach and kidneys.

Smoking is also linked to some types of leukaemia (cancer of the white blood cells).

Your heart and circulation

Smoking damages your blood vessels and increases your risk of getting heart disease and of having a stroke.

Smoking can also affect how well your blood flows around your body. You may get cold hands and feet, which is a result of not enough blood getting to them.

Your lungs

It's hardly surprising that if you're regularly breathing in smoke, your airways can get damaged. It can become harder for you to get air in to and out of your lungs and you might develop chronic obstructive pulmonary disease (COPD).

Smoking can also put you at risk of complications if you get the flu.

Your appearance

The tar in cigarettes stains your fingers and teeth, so they become discoloured and yellow.

Smoking also reduces your sense of taste and smell.

Your fertility

Men who smoke are likely to have fewer sperm. The sperm are also more likely to be damaged so they are less able to fertilise an egg. You're also at a greater risk of erectile dysfunction if you smoke.

On average, women who smoke go through the menopause a year and a half earlier than women who don't smoke.

Your recovery from operations

If you smoke and need an operation – whether it's related to smoking or not – your body will take longer to heal afterwards. Your risk of getting complications is higher too. This means a longer recovery period with more time in hospital and off work.

Key facts

Cigarette smoke contains at least 4,000 chemical compounds and of these, more than 40 are known to cause cancer.

Although people often think that hand-rolled cigarettes are healthier because they are more 'natural', it's a myth. Hand-rolled cigarettes are just as harmful as manufactured ones.

Key facts

If you smoke 20 or more cigarettes a day, your risk of having a stroke can be up to six times that of a non-smoker.

If you're under 50 and smoke, you're five times more likely to have a heart attack than a non-smoker.

Nearly nine out of ten people who get COPD are smokers.

Children of parents who smoke are more likely to get asthma or other breathing problems.

Smoking can prematurely age you by ten years or more, and you're more likely to get wrinkles on your face at a younger age.

Smokers are three times as likely to take over a year to get pregnant than non-smokers.

Smoking can affect how successful fertility treatment such as in vitro fertilisation (IVF) is.

Smoking is the biggest risk factor for getting serious complications after having a hip or knee replacement.

If you smoke, you're much more at risk of getting complications during reconstructive breast surgery and breast cancer surgery.

Why smoking is bad for people around you

People around you will be passive smoking when they breathe in your smoke – this carries all the same health risks as smoking.

Short-term effects

Being exposed to second-hand smoke is very unpleasant – it can give you a headache, cough or sore throat. It can also irritate your eyes and make you feel sick or dizzy. If you have asthma, being in a smoky place may make your symptoms worse. And add the irritation of the smell of smoke on your clothes and hair. All in all, smokers can be seriously unpopular.

Long-term effects

If you're regularly exposed to second-hand smoke, your risk of developing smoking-related diseases such as heart disease and lung cancer increases. Not only that, you're more likely to develop conditions that affect your breathing, such as chronic obstructive pulmonary disease (COPD).

Passive smoking in pregnancy

If you're exposed to second-hand smoke while you're pregnant, your baby may not develop properly before birth and may have a low birth weight. Women who passive smoke while they're pregnant may have an increased risk of stillbirth too.

Passive smoking in children

Passive smoking has a number of effects in children – it may reduce their mental development, for example. They're also more likely to get:

⇨ asthma – and being in a smoky place may make their symptoms worse

⇨ glue ear, or a middle ear infection

⇨ attention deficit hyperactivity disorder (ADHD).

Children who grow up with parents or siblings who smoke are almost twice as likely to become smokers themselves.

⇨ The above information is reprinted with kind permission from Bupa. Please visit www.bupa.co.uk for further information.

© 2018 Bupa

Tobacco

Key facts

⇨ Tobacco kills up to half of its users.

⇨ Tobacco kills more than seven million people each year. More than six million of those deaths are the result of direct tobacco use while around 890,000 are the result of non-smokers being exposed to second-hand smoke.

⇨ Around 80% of the world's 1.1 billion smokers live in low- and middle-income countries.

Leading cause of death, illness and impoverishment

The tobacco epidemic is one of the biggest public health threats the world has ever faced, killing more than 7 million people a year. More than six million of those deaths are the result of direct tobacco use while around 890,000 are the result of non-smokers, being exposed to second-hand smoke.

Around 80% of the 1.1 billion smokers worldwide live in low- and middle-income countries, where the burden of tobacco-related illness and death is heaviest.

Tobacco users who die prematurely deprive their families of income, raise the cost of health care and hinder economic development.

In some countries, children from poor households are frequently employed in tobacco farming to provide family income. These children are especially vulnerable to 'green tobacco sickness', which is caused by the nicotine that is absorbed through the skin from the handling of wet tobacco leaves.

Surveillance is key

Good monitoring tracks the extent and character of the tobacco epidemic and indicates how best to tailor policies. Only one in three countries, representing 39% of the world's population, monitors tobacco use by repeating nationally representative youth and adult surveys at least once every five years.

Second-hand smoke kills

Second-hand smoke is the smoke that fills restaurants, offices or other enclosed spaces when people burn tobacco products such as cigarettes, bidis and water-pipes. There are more than 4,000 chemicals in tobacco smoke, of which at least 250 are known to be harmful and more than 50 are known to cause cancer.

There is no safe level of exposure to second-hand tobacco smoke.

⇨ In adults, second-hand smoke causes serious cardiovascular and respiratory diseases, including coronary heart disease and lung cancer. In infants, it causes sudden death. In pregnant women, it causes low birth weight.

⇨ Almost half of children regularly breathe air polluted by tobacco smoke in public places.

⇨ Second-hand smoke causes more than 890,000 premature deaths per year.

⇨ In 2004, children accounted for 28% of the deaths attributable to second-hand smoke.

Every person should be able to breathe tobacco-smoke-free air. Smoke-free laws protect the health of non-smokers, are popular, do not harm business and encourage smokers to quit.

Over 1.4 billion people, or 20% of the world's population, are protected by comprehensive national smoke-free laws.

Tobacco users need help to quit

Studies show that few people understand the specific health risks of tobacco use. For example, a 2009 survey in China revealed that only 38% of smokers knew that smoking causes coronary heart disease and only 27% knew that it causes stroke.

Among smokers who are aware of the dangers of tobacco, most want to quit. Counselling and medication can more than double the chance that a smoker who tries to quit will succeed.

National comprehensive cessation services with full or partial cost-coverage are available to assist tobacco users to quit in only 26 countries, representing 33% of the world's population.

Picture warnings work

Hard-hitting anti-tobacco advertisements and graphic pack warnings – especially those that include pictures – reduce the number of children who begin smoking and increase the number of smokers who quit.

Graphic warnings can persuade smokers to protect the health of non-smokers by smoking less inside the home and avoiding smoking near children. Studies carried out after the implementation of pictorial package warnings in Brazil, Canada, Singapore and Thailand consistently show that pictorial warnings significantly increase people's awareness of the harms of tobacco use.

Only 78 countries, representing 47% of the world's population, meet the best practice for pictorial warnings, which includes the warnings in the local language and cover an average of at least half of the front and back of cigarette packs.

Mass media campaigns can also reduce tobacco consumption by influencing people to protect non-smokers and convincing youths to stop using tobacco.

Around 44% of the world's population live in the 43 countries that have aired at least one strong anti-tobacco mass media campaign within the last two years.

Ad bans lower consumption

Bans on tobacco advertising, promotion and sponsorship can reduce tobacco consumption.

A comprehensive ban on all tobacco advertising, promotion and sponsorship could decrease tobacco consumption by an average of about 7%, with some countries experiencing a decline in consumption of up to 16%.

Only 37 countries, representing 15% of the world's population, have completely banned all forms of tobacco advertising, promotion and sponsorship.

Taxes discourage tobacco use

Tobacco taxes are the most cost-effective way to reduce tobacco use, especially among young and poor people. A tax increase that increases

tobacco prices by 10% decreases tobacco consumption by about 4% in high-income countries and about 5% in low- and middle-income countries.

Even so, high tobacco taxes is a measure that is rarely implemented. Only 32 countries, with 10% of the world's population, have introduced taxes on tobacco products so that more than 75% of the retail price is tax. Tobacco tax revenues are on average 250 times higher than spending on tobacco control, based on available data.

Illicit trade of tobacco products must be stopped

The illicit trade in tobacco products poses major health, economic and security concerns around the world. It is estimated that one in every ten cigarettes and tobacco products consumed globally is illicit. The illicit market is supported by various players, ranging from petty peddlers to organised criminal networks involved in arms and human trafficking.

Tax avoidance (licit) and tax evasion (illicit) undermine the effectiveness of tobacco control policies, particularly higher tobacco taxes. These activities range from legal actions, such as purchasing tobacco products in lower tax jurisdictions, to illegal ones such as smuggling, illicit manufacturing and counterfeiting.

The tobacco industry and others often argue that high tobacco product taxes lead to tax evasion. However, the evidence shows that non-tax factors including weak governance, high levels of corruption, poor government commitment to tackling illicit tobacco, ineffective customs and tax administration, and informal distribution channels for tobacco products are often of equal or greater importance.

There is broad agreement that control of illicit trade benefits tobacco control and public health and result in broader benefits for governments. Critically, this will reduce premature deaths from tobacco use and raise tax revenue for governments. Stopping illicit trade in tobacco products is a health priority, and is achievable. But to do so requires improvement of national and sub-national tax administration systems and international collaboration. The WHO FCTC Protocol to Eliminate the Illicit Trade of Tobacco Products (ITP) is the key supply side policy to reduce tobacco use and its health and economic consequences.

While publicly stating its support for action against the illicit trade, the tobacco industry's behind-the-scenes behaviour has been very different. Internal industry documents released as a result of court cases demonstrate that the tobacco industry has actively fostered the illicit trade globally. It also works to block implementation of tobacco control measures, such as tax increases and pictorial health warnings, by misleadingly arguing they will fuel the illicit trade.

Experience from many countries demonstrate that illicit trade can be successfully addressed even when tobacco taxes and prices are raised, resulting in increased tax revenues and reduced tobacco use. Implementing and enforcing strong measures to control illicit trade enhances the effectiveness of significantly increased tobacco taxes and prices, as well as strong tobacco control policies, in reducing tobacco use and its health and economic consequences.

WHO response

WHO is committed to fighting the global tobacco epidemic. The WHO Framework Convention on Tobacco Control (WHO FCTC) entered into force in February 2005 and has today 181 Parties covering more than 90% of the world's population.

The WHO FCTC is a milestone in the promotion of public health. It is an evidence-based treaty that reaffirms the right of people to the highest standard of health, provides legal dimensions for international health cooperation and sets high standards for compliance.

In 2008, WHO introduced a practical, cost-effective way to scale up implementation of the main demand reduction provisions of the WHO FCTC on the ground: MPOWER. Each MPOWER measure corresponds to at least one provision of the WHO Framework Convention on Tobacco Control.

The six MPOWER measures are:

⇨ Monitor tobacco use and prevention policies

⇨ Protect people from tobacco use

⇨ Offer help to quit tobacco use

⇨ Warn about the dangers of tobacco

⇨ Enforce bans on tobacco advertising, promotion and sponsorship

⇨ Raise taxes on tobacco.

2017

⇨ The above information is reprinted with kind permission from WHO. Please visit www.who.int for further information.

The impact of active and passive smoking upon health and neurocognitive function

The Editorial on the Research Topic.

The impact of active and passive smoking upon health and neurocognitive function.

By Tom Heffeman, Department of Psychology, Northumbria University, Newcastle-upon-Tyne, UK

Tobacco smoking is a major risk factor for a number of chronic diseases, including a variety of cancers, lung disease, and damage to the cardiovascular system. The World Health Organization recently calculated that there were six million smoking-attributable deaths per year and that this number is due to rise to about eight million per year by the end of 2030. Recent work has demonstrated that habitual smoking in adults is associated with a range of health conditions, including cardiovascular disease, pulmonary dysfunction, and an increased risk of a variety of cancers. In terms of neurocognitive function, although some studies have found that acute smoking can enhance cognitive functions in the short term, actually chronic smoking is deleterious in the long term. Chronic smoking has been associated with reductions in working memory (the temporary storage and manipulation of information), executive function (planning tasks, focusing one's attention, and ignoring irrelevant distractions), and prospective memory (memory for everyday things, such as keeping an appointment, or taking an important medication on time). More recently, the focus on smoking-related health problems and neurocognitive deficits has expanded to include the study of 'second-hand smoking' (also known as 'passive smoking' – wherein a person who does not smoke him/herself inhales tobacco smoke either via side-stream smoke or via smoke being blown directly into his/her face). Research in this area has linked exposure to second-hand smoke in those who have never smoked to a range of health problems akin to smokers, including lung and cardiovascular disease, as well as deficits in neurocognitive function. In terms of neurocognitive function, exposure to second-hand smoke has been linked with an increased risk of mild cognitive impairments in older adults, reductions in working memory, as well as deficits in executive function. Interventions aimed at reducing cigarette consumption and improving the health of both smokers and those exposed to second-hand smoke continue to be developed. The aim of this Frontiers Research Topic is to bring together a collection of papers that look at what impact active and passive smoking has upon health and neurocognitive function; as well as to consider some of the wide variety of interventions aimed at reducing cigarette use and/or improving health.

Copeland examined pre-treatment characteristics among daily smokers (including smoking patterns, smoking outcome expectancies, and smoking-related health information) and how these related to success on a brief motivational enhancement intervention. Marshall et al. explored whether the combined (polydrug) effect of consuming excessive amounts of alcohol and smoking cigarettes exacerbated everyday memory problems when compared with the sum of their independent effects (excessive drinking alone, or smoking alone). Philibert et al.

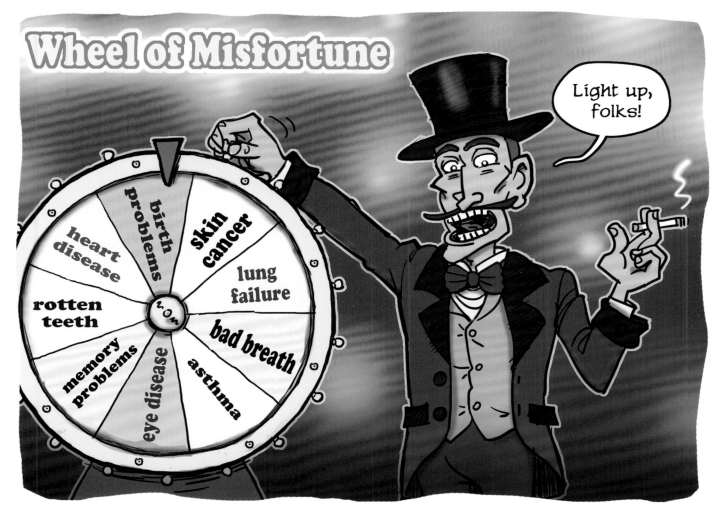

examined whether aryl hydrocarbon receptor repressor (AHRR) can be used to determine whether AHRR methylation status is a quantifiable biomarker for progress in smoking cessation that could have substantial impact on both smoking cessation treatment and research. Ling and Heffernan reviewed evidence in relation to the cognitive consequences of exposure to second-hand smoke in those who had no history of smoking. Payne et al. evaluated chronic obstructive pulmonary disease-related health factors in flight attendants exposed to second-hand cigarette smoke and assessed whether meditative movement was effective as a treatment in improving pulmonary function in these flight attendants. Jukosky et al. demonstrated how cigarette exposure alters the innate immune response and increases an individual's susceptibility to pathogen infection when compared with non-exposed individuals. Jovanovic and Jakovljevic discuss regulatory control of e-cigarette composition and raises concern regarding the quality control

and health outcomes surrounding e-cigarettes. The commentary by Parrott discusses concerns about the paradoxical nature of using e-cigarettes; whether they may in fact be damaging to physical/psychological health of the users, as well as raising concerns about what impact e-cigarettes have upon those who are 'passively vaping.' Lasebikan and Ola assessed the efficacy of screening, brief intervention, and referral for treatment package to reduce tobacco smoking in two semi-rural community settings in South-West Nigeria.

Overall, the papers presented in *Frontiers in Psychiatry* special topic demonstrates the broad nature of research currently being undertaken in relation to active and passive smoking and some of the current issues surrounding the use of e-cigarettes as nicotine-replacement therapy. The research cited here should pave the way for further work in this area. Areas for future research include the concern of what impact

exposure to second-hand smoke might be having upon children's health, neurocognitive function, and educational achievement, an area of particular importance given the recent estimates from the World Health Organization that approximately 40% of children across the world are regularly exposed to second-hand smoke in the home. A further area that has received very little attention at all is whether exposure to 'third-hand smoke' (the residue of nicotine and other chemicals left on indoor surfaces as a result of tobacco smoking) has a detrimental impact upon those who have never smoked, both in terms of health and neurocognitive function.

29 August 2016

⇨ The above information is reprinted with kind permission from NCBI. Please visit www.ncbi.nlm.nih.gov for further information.

Diagnosed autism linked to maternal grandmother's smoking in pregnancy

Scientists from the University of Bristol have looked at all 14,500 participants in 'Children of the 90s' and found that if a girl's maternal grandmother smoked during pregnancy, the girl is 67 per cent more likely to display certain traits linked to autism, such as poor social communication skills and repetitive behaviours.

The team also found that if the maternal grandmother smoked, this increased by 53 per cent the risk of her grandchildren having a diagnosed autism spectrum disorder (ASD).

These discoveries suggest that if a female is exposed to cigarette smoke while she is still in the womb, it could affect the developing eggs – causing changes that may eventually affect the development of her own children. Further research is now needed to find out what these molecular changes might be, and to see whether the same associations are present in other groups of people.

Unlike the analysis of autistic traits, which was based on over 7,000 participants, the 177 diagnosed with ASD were too few to analyse grandsons and granddaughters separately.

The discovery, published today in *Scientific Reports*, is part of an ongoing, long-term study of the effects of maternal and paternal grandmother's smoking in pregnancy on the development of their grandchildren, who are all part of Children of the 90s. By using detailed information collected over many years on multiple factors that may affect children's health and development, the researchers were able to rule out other potential explanations for their results.

The incidence of ASD has increased in recent years, and while some of this increase is undoubtedly down to improved diagnosis, changes in environment or lifestyle are also likely to play a role. The researchers also stress that many different factors, including genetic variation, are believed to affect an individual's chances of developing ASD.

Past studies of maternal smoking in pregnancy and ASD in children have been inconclusive. Going back a generation has revealed an intergenerational effect, which interestingly is most clear cut when the mother herself did not smoke in pregnancy.

The reasons for this are not entirely clear but Professor Marcus Pembrey, one of the paper's authors, said: "In terms of mechanisms, there are two broad possibilities. There is DNA damage that is transmitted to the grandchildren or there is some adaptive response to the smoking that leaves the grandchild more vulnerable to ASD. We have no explanation for the sex difference, although we have previously found that grand-maternal smoking is associated with different growth patterns in grandsons and granddaughters.

"More specifically, we know smoking can damage the DNA of mitochondria – the numerous 'power-packs' contained in every cell, and mitochondria are only transmitted to the next generation via the mother's egg. The initial mitochondrial DNA mutations often have no overt effect in the mother herself, but the impact can increase when transmitted to her own children."

Professor Jean Golding, another author, added: "We already know that protecting a baby from tobacco smoke is one of the best things a woman can do to give her child a healthy start in life. Now we've found that not smoking during pregnancy could also give their future grandchildren a better start too. We have started studying the next generation of participants (COCO90s), so eventually we will be able to see if the effect carries down from the great-grandparents to their great-grandchildren too."

Dr Dheeraj Rai, another author, added: "We still do not know why many children develop autism and behaviours linked to it. The associations we observe raise intriguing issues on possible transgenerational influences in autism. Future research will help understand the meaning and mechanisms behind these findings. The National Autistic Society website contains a wealth of information about autism and details on how and where to seek advice."

Alycia Halladay, PhD, chief science officer at the Autism Science Foundation (USA), said: "To date, research into the causes of autism has been limited to studying maternal or paternal exposures during pregnancy. By utilising a birth cohort in the United Kingdom [Children of the 90s], scientists are able to go back a generation to examine the role of grandparental exposures, presumably through germline mutations and epigenetic modifications. Hopefully, grandparental exposures will continue to be investigated to better understand this mechanism."

27 April 2017

⇨ The above information is reprinted with kind permission from the University of Bristol. Please visit www.bristol.ac.uk for further information.

Illegal tobacco is bought by more than half of teenage smokers in Gateshead

Figures show children are regular customers of dealers as new campaign is launched.

Illegal tobacco has helped over half of underage smokers in the North East get hooked on smoking, a new survey released today suggests.

55% of children aged 14 and 15 who smoke say they buy illegal tobacco from sources like 'tab houses' and shops – while 73% say they have been offered illegal tobacco.

The figures, from the 2017 North East Illegal Tobacco Survey, are released as Fresh launches the new 'Keep It Out' campaign aimed at helping the public to spot illegal tobacco, report it and to encourage smokers not to buy it.

As well as helping children to start smoking, people supplying illegal tobacco are often involved in drugs or loan sharking. Buying it means supporting crime and can bring children into contact with criminals.

Ailsa Rutter, Director of Fresh, said: "One in two smokers will die from their addiction, and no-one wants their child to start.

"While fewer people than ever are now smoking, illegal cigarettes are often responsible for getting children initiated on smoking as they can buy it at pocket money prices from people who don't care who they sell to."

Peter Wright, from the North East Public Protection Partnership, said: "People might think they are getting a bargain, but illegal cigarettes come at a very high cost to local communities and buying it means supporting it.

"A lot of people kid themselves they're buying duty free. But the trade is linked to organised crime and at the top are organised criminals with UK smokers in their sights. Local criminals also regularly come into neighbourhoods to supply their dealers.

"Even if you don't think local sellers are selling to kids, many are, and there is strong intelligence of kids in school uniforms buying from tab houses.

"Whether people smoke or not, we're urging people to do something about it and report it anonymously."

Councillor Linda Green, Cabinet Member for Communities and Volunteering, Gateshead Council, said: "This campaign is about raising awareness of the harm illicit tobacco does to our local communities. Not only are children and young people targeted by people who sell illegal cigarettes but it also brings crime into our neighbourhoods. We will continue to work with Northumbria Police and our communities to try to limit the impact of illegal tobacco."

Alice Wiseman, Director of Public Health, Gateshead Council, said: "Tackling tobacco use is a top priority for us as smoking kills one person in Gateshead every 21 hours. Even though it is such a dangerous product,

at the moment anyone can sell it. The availability of illegal tobacco is undermining the work we're trying to do as cheaper tobacco means people are less likely to quit and it also makes it easily accessible to children. We strongly believe selling tobacco should be licensed in the same way as selling alcohol so we can more effectively protect people from tobacco harms."

Anyone with information about houses, shops, pubs or individuals selling illegal tobacco can give information online at www.keep-it-out.co.uk or by calling the illegal tobacco hotline at 0300 999 00 00. All information will be treated anonymously.

The survey of over 3,000 people from across the North East, which has tracked the size of the illegal tobacco market since 2009 and attitudes towards it, has found in 2017:

- Illicit makes up 12% of all tobacco smoked – a smaller proportion than in 2009 (16%) but slightly higher than in 2015 (9%).

- Less than one in five (18%) of smokers buy illicit – a reduction from 24% in 2009.

- The proportion of smokers who have tried illicit tobacco has decreased from 46% in 2011 to 37% in 2017.

- Those smokers who do buy illegal tobacco are buying more of it – it makes up 58% of their overall tobacco compared to 40% in 2013.

- Private addresses are the leading source (42%) followed by shops (24%).

- Less is now being bought in pubs – but pubs are still the place where smokers are most likely to be offered it by hawkers touting it around.

Shopkeeper John McClurey, a former North of England President of the National Federation of Retail Newsagents, said: "Most retailers would not dream of stocking illegal tobacco or selling to children, and are very angry about the illegal tobacco trade. The figures are concerning.

"There is a strong case for tougher penalties against those who sell it as a deterrent and to weed out the few bad apples in the retail trade without conscience."

Fresh is calling on the Government to introduce a licensing system for tobacco manufacturers and retailers to provide funding for improved enforcement and other measures to reduce smoking prevalence. The measure would be popular in the North East with 76% of adults strongly in favour of businesses needing a valid licence to sell tobacco.

1 November 2017

- The above information is reprinted with kind permission from Gateshead Council. Please visit www.gateshead.gov.uk for further information.

Tobacco-smoke residue that lingers in furniture, curtains and house dust can still be harmful

THE CONVERSATION

An article from **The Conversation.**

By Jacqueline Hamilton, reader in Atmospheric Chemistry, University of York

Mice exposed to household fabrics contaminated with third-hand tobacco smoke showed changes in biological markers of health after only one month, a recent study found. After six months, the mice showed evidence of liver damage and insulin resistance, symptoms which usually precede the development of type 2 diabetes.

Each year about 600,000 people die from exposure to second-hand tobacco smoke (inhaling other people's cigarette smoke). Once the smoke clears, after a cigarette has been extinguished, nicotine and other harmful chemicals left behind can stick to surfaces and fabrics. This residue is known as third-hand smoke.

The idea of third-hand smoke has been around for a few decades, but

came to prominence in 2009 after a study by Jonathan Winickoff, an assistant professor of paediatrics at Harvard Medical School, identified a link between parents' belief that third-hand smoke may cause harm and the likelihood they would prohibit smoking within their home.

There is growing evidence that third-hand smoke contamination is extensive and can linger for extended periods. Non-smokers can be exposed to third-hand smoke from breathing residual gases, touching surfaces and swallowing dust. Chemical reactions of nicotine stuck to surfaces can lead to an increase in the amount of carcinogenic chemicals over time.

A landmark study in 2011 by Georg Matt of San Diego State University showed that nicotine levels were still elevated in house dust in non-smokers' homes two months after the previous smoking tenants vacated. Even infants in a neonatal intensive-care unit in the US, with a strict no-smoking policy, had chemical markers of tobacco exposure in their urine after a visit from a parent who smoked.

The link between smoking and ill health, including cancer, is now well established, but what about the impact of third-hand smoke on non-smokers? There has been considerable effort in recent years to determine whether or not third-hand smoke is toxic to humans.

What the new study adds

The new mouse model study investigated the effects of third-hand smoke exposure over time on animal health (the first study to do so). The researchers, from the University of California, Riverside, used a smoking machine to create third-hand smoke-contaminated household fabrics in mice cages, including curtain material, upholstery and carpet. Once the fabrics showed levels likely to be found in smokers' homes, the mice were placed in the cage and monitored over a period of six months.

After just one month, the mice showed changes in markers of health in the blood serum, liver and brain tissues. The range and severity of the changes on the health of mice got progressively worse the longer they were exposed.

After four months, the mice showed increases in factors related to oxidative stress and liver damage. Fasting glucose and insulin levels increased with third-hand smoke exposure and, after four months, the mice already had a increased risk of type 2 diabetes.

The speed at which third-hand smoke residues cause measurable health effects in the mice is surprising. How the health effects observed in mice translate to humans, though, remains an open question.

Greater risk for children

The authors suggest that since humans mature slower than mice, the exposure times may need to be longer before biological changes can be observed. Unlike the idealised mouse experiment, where they spent all of their life with the third-hand-smoke materials, children and adults will be exposed to different third-hand smoke levels throughout the day.

In the mouse experiments, inhalation or absorption of third-hand smoke residues through the skin were the main exposure methods. But children could also ingest third-hand smoke from house dust – something the mice weren't exposed to in the study.

Children, particularly toddlers, are at greater risk from contaminated dust because they spend more time close to the ground and are more likely to put materials in their mouths.

Using measurements of third-hand smoke constituents in house dust from 80 Spanish homes, we found that for children aged one to six years old, the cancer risks from exposure exceeded the limit recommended by the US Environmental Protection Agency (EPA) in three-quarters of smokers' homes and two-thirds of non-smokers' homes.

We can usually smell third-hand smoke on the clothing of smokers, or when we enter a room where a cigarette has been smoked. But it is clear that low levels of tobacco residues can contaminate homes without our knowledge. This study adds to growing evidence that third-hand smoke can have serious long-term health consequences for non-smokers, particularly children.

The Californian Consortium on Thirdhand Smoke recently reviewed the evidence on third-hand smoke, showing a range of harmful effects. Recent studies have shown that exposure to third-hand smoke can damage DNA and cells, and cause metabolism and behavioural changes.

18 September 2017

⇨ The above information is reprinted with kind permission from *The Conversation*. Please visit www.theconversation.com for further information.

PHE publishes independent expert e-cigarettes evidence review

A new Public Health England (PHE) e-cigarette evidence review, undertaken by leading independent tobacco experts, provides an update on PHE's 2015 review.

The report covers e-cigarette use among young people and adults, public attitudes, the impact on quitting smoking, an update on risks to health and the role of nicotine. It also reviews heated tobacco products.

The main findings of PHE's evidence review are that:

⇨ vaping poses only a small fraction of the risks of smoking and switching completely from smoking to vaping conveys substantial health benefits

⇨ e-cigarettes could be contributing to at least 20,000 successful new quits per year and possibly many more

⇨ e-cigarette use is associated with improved quit success rates over the last year and an accelerated drop in smoking rates across the country

⇨ many thousands of smokers incorrectly believe that vaping is as harmful as smoking; around 40% of smokers have not even tried an e-cigarette

⇨ there is much public misunderstanding about nicotine (less than 10% of adults understand that most of the harms to health from smoking are not caused by nicotine)

⇨ the use of e-cigarettes in the UK has plateaued over the last few years at just under three million

⇨ the evidence does not support the concern that e-cigarettes are a route into smoking among young people (youth smoking rates in the UK continue to decline, regular use is rare and is almost entirely confined to those who have smoked).

PHE's evidence review comes just a few weeks after a US National Academies of Sciences, Engineering and Medicine report on e-cigarettes. Their conclusion on e-cigarette safety also finds that based on the available evidence "e-cigarettes are likely to be far less harmful than combustible tobacco cigarettes".

Professor John Newton, Director for Health Improvement at PHE said:

⇨ Every minute someone is admitted to hospital from smoking, with around 79,000 deaths a year in England alone.

⇨ Our new review reinforces the finding that vaping is a fraction of the risk of smoking, at least 95% less harmful, and of negligible risk to bystanders. Yet over half of smokers either falsely believe that vaping is as harmful as smoking or just don't know.

⇨ It would be tragic if thousands of smokers who could quit with the help of an e-cigarette are being put off due to false fears about their safety.

Professor Ann McNeill, lead author and Professor of Tobacco Addiction at King's College London said:

⇨ It's of great concern that smokers still have such a poor understanding about what causes the harm from smoking. When people smoke tobacco cigarettes, they inhale a lethal mix of 7,000 smoke constituents, 70 of which are known to cause cancer.

⇨ People smoke for the nicotine, but contrary to what the vast majority believe, nicotine causes little if any of the harm. The toxic smoke is the culprit and is the overwhelming cause of all the tobacco-related disease and death. There are now a greater variety of alternative ways of getting nicotine than ever before, including nicotine gum, nasal spray, lozenges and e-cigarettes.

Professor Linda Bauld, author and Professor of Health Policy, University of Stirling and Chair in Behavioural Research for Cancer Prevention, Cancer Research UK said:

⇨ Concern has been expressed that e-cigarette use will lead young people into smoking. But in the UK, research clearly shows that regular use of e-cigarettes among young people who have never smoked remains negligible, less than 1%, and youth smoking continues to decline at an encouraging rate. We need to keep closely monitoring these trends, but so far the data suggest that e-cigarettes are not acting as a route into regular smoking amongst young people.

PHE is calling on smokers and a number of bodies to act on the evidence.

Smokers

Anyone who has struggled to quit should try switching to an e-cigarette and get professional help. The greatest quit success is among those who combine using an e-cigarette with support from a local stop smoking service.

Local stop smoking services and healthcare professionals

These should provide behavioural support to those smokers wanting to quit with the help of an e-cigarette. A new training course on e-cigarettes for healthcare professionals by the National Centre for Smoking Cessation and Training is now live.

Medicines and Healthcare products Regulatory Agency (MHRA)

MHRA continue their work in regulating and licensing e-cigarette products and support manufacturers to expedite the licensing of e-cigarettes as medicinal quit aids. PHE believes there is compelling evidence that e-cigarettes be made available to NHS patients.

NHS Trusts

To become truly smokefree, Trusts should ensure

⇨ e-cigarettes, alongside nicotine replacement therapies are available for sale in hospital shops

⇨ vaping policies support smokers to quit and stay smokefree

⇨ smoking shelters be removed

⇨ frontline staff take every opportunity to encourage and support patients to quit.

The government's new Tobacco Control Plan for England includes a commitment to 'maximise the availability of safer alternatives to smoking'. It makes clear that e-cigarettes have an important part to play in achieving the ambition for a smokefree generation.

Background
Read the report commissioned by PHE – Evidence review of e-cigarettes and heated tobacco products – McNeill A, Brose LS, Calder R, Bauld L & Robson D (2018).
Over the past few years, e-cigarette use has hovered at just under 6% of the adult population in Britain. The most common reason for e-cigarette use continues to be to help with quitting and they are the most popular quitting tool in England. At the same time, quit success rates have been improving and we are also seeing an accelerated drop in smoking rates (currently 15.5% in England): smokinginengland.info/latest-statistics.
79,000 people in England die every year as a result of smoking, and over half of long-term smokers will die from a smoking-related illness if they do not quit: digital.nhs.uk/catalogue/PUB24228.
PHE 2015 e-cigarettes evidence review: McNeill A., P. Hajek et al, E-cigarettes – an evidence update: A report commissioned by Public Health England, Public Health England, August. Authors' note on evidence for 'around 95% safer' estimate.
Nicotine without smoke: tobacco harm reduction, Royal College of Physicians, April 2016.
Smoking Toolkit Study.
ASH (May 2017) Use of e-cigarettes (vapourisers) among adults in Great Britain.
Bauld, Linda, Anne Marie MacKintosh, Brian Eastwood, Allison Ford, Graham Moore, Martin Dockrell, Deborah Arnott, Hazel Cheeseman, and Ann McNeill. 'Young people's use of e-cigarettes across the United Kingdom: Findings from five surveys 2015–2017.' International journal of environmental research and public health 14, no. 9 (2017): 973.
Towards a Smokefree Generation: A Tobacco Control Plan for England Department of Health, July 2017.
NHS Digital, Statistics on Smoking: England, 2017.
US National Academies of Sciences, Engineering, and Medicine (January 2018) Public Health Consequences of E-Cigarettes.

6 February 2018

⇨ The above information is reprinted with kind permission from GOV. UK. Please visit www.gov.uk for further information.

Nearly half of teenage smokers have bought illegal tobacco, so what are the dangers?

***An article from* The Conversation.**

THE CONVERSATION

By Andrew Russell, Associate Professor and Fellow of the Wolfson Research Institute for Health and Wellbeing, Durham University

New figures show that more than half of all teenage smokers in the north-east of England have bought illegal tobacco.

The figures, from the 2017 North East Illegal Tobacco Survey, found that 55% of children aged 14 and 15 who smoke say they buy illegal tobacco from shops or "tab houses" – while 73% say they have been offered illegal tobacco at some point.

Illegal tobacco is either smuggled, counterfeit (fake), bootlegged or illegally manufactured. It is generally much cheaper than legal tobacco and can be a serious deterrent to people deciding to give up smoking.

These latest findings highlight how as well as adults, illegal tobacco harms young people too. There have even been cases of illicit tobacco being sold to children from ice-cream vans. And sometimes these sales are for single sticks – which are much easier for kids to buy with their pocket money.

Here's what you need to know about those illegal cigarettes

1. Illegal cigarettes are just as harmful as normal ones

All cigarettes are harmful to health. And all tobacco, whether legal or illegal, contains over 4,000 chemicals. A High Court judgement in 2016 recognised there is no difference in the harm presented by any brand of tobacco. In this way, tobacco control advocates often liken any differences between legal and illegal tobacco to the choice between jumping out of the 12th or 13th floor of a burning building.

2. Tobacco smuggling has been linked to terrorism

Although the illicit tobacco market in the UK is complex and fast-changing, many cases that come to the courts are linked to other activities such as drug dealing, alcohol and even people trafficking. Illicit tobacco has also been linked to organised crime and even the funding of terrorism. In this way illicit tobacco sales bring criminal activity right onto people's streets and doorsteps.

3. Normal cigarette factories can be in on the act

On top of well-known brands smuggled from one country to another, there can also be counterfeit (fake) tobacco products and so-called "cheap whites". These are new brands of cigarettes manufactured in one country but intended mainly for illegal sale in another. Illegal manufacturing of tobacco often takes place in either regular factories out-of-hours, or in secret operations capable of producing millions of cigarettes a day.

4. Tobacco firms have historically been complicit in smuggling

There is plenty of evidence to show that tobacco companies have been complicit in tobacco smuggling. This is a situation that appears to persist in many low and middle income countries. After all, it doesn't matter to tobacco companies whether their products are sold 'tax paid' or 'tax free' – and if the latter means they sell more, then that's so many more people hooked.

5. But the good news is that illegal tobacco use is declining

Despite some spurious reports, statistics from HM Revenue & Customs show that the illegal tobacco now makes up just 13% of the overall tobacco market – compared to 21% in 2000. Latest estimates also show that just 10% of cigarettes in Britain today are sold illegally, though the figure is higher at 39% for hand-rolling tobacco.

An EU products directive, which came into force in 2016, includes a 'tracking and tracing' system that will make it much easier to identify supply chains and the legal status of tobacco on sale in the UK. But of course, that won't immediately help the teenagers getting hooked on illegal tobacco.

20 November 2017

⇨ The above information is reprinted with kind permission from *The Conversation*. Please visit www.theconversation.com for further information.

E-cigarettes potentially as harmful as tobacco cigarettes, says study

The evidence isn't looking good.

By Sophie Gallagher

The global e-cigarette market is set to be worth $32 billion by 2021, and with the UK share reaching almost $6 billion, this alternative to tobacco cigarettes is increasingly popular among smokers.

But the research into the health implications, and dangers, of electronic cigarettes, are still much debated by medical scientists.

Now a new study has added to the growing evidence that e-cigarettes, or vaping, is not as harmless as was once hoped, and in fact could be on par with the damage done by inhaling unfiltered tobacco.

The study from the University of Connecticut found that e-cigarettes, loaded with nicotine-based liquid, are potentially as harmful when it comes to causing cellular mutations and DNA damage.

Changes which may lead to diseases such as cancer.

The amount of damage depends on the amount of vapour the user inhales, the other additives present, whether nicotine or non-nicotine liquid is used.

Karteek Kadimisetty, a researcher and the study's lead author said: "Some people use e-cigarettes heavily because they think there is no harm. We wanted to see exactly what might be happening to DNA, and we had the resources in our lab to do that."

They found that the potential DNA damage from e-cigarettes increased with the number of puffs, and speculate that this damage is a result of the many chemical additives added to e-cigarettes and present in the vapours.

The ingredients usually present in e-cigs are propylene glycol, glycerine, nicotine and other flavourings.

The study seems to contradict advice given by Public Health England (PHE) last year, which said vaping is 95% less harmful than tobacco. At the time, PHE called for GPs to be able to prescribe e-cigarettes on the NHS to help people quit smoking.

Frequently viewed as a less toxic alternative for people looking to break their habit of smoking tobacco cigarettes, modern e-cigarettes have steadily risen in popularity since they first appeared on the commercial market in 2004.

Back in 2016, a study also showed that vaping is as bad for heart health as smoking, as the average vaping session caused similar damage to the heart and aorta.

12 June 2017

⇨ The above information is reprinted with kind permission from The Huffington Post UK. Please visit www.huffingtonpost.co.uk for further information.

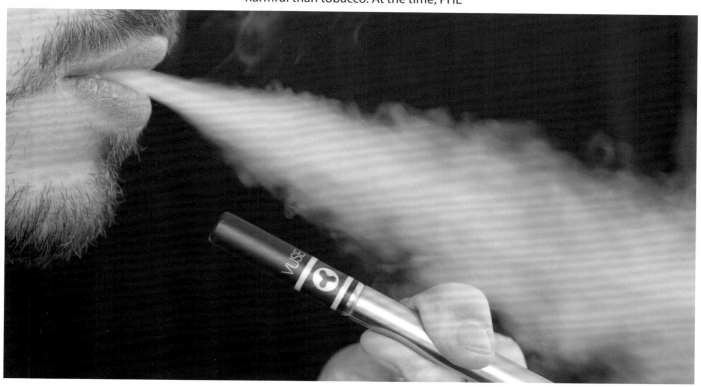

Police fail to fine a single driver for smoking with children in car under new law as officers 'turn blind eye'

By Danny Boyle

Police are not enforcing a new law to protect children from adults smoking in cars, it has emerged, as figures showed no one has been fined since legislation was introduced.

Since October last year, anyone caught smoking in a vehicle carrying someone under the age of 18 has been breaking the law and could face a £50 fine.

The clampdown was introduced by the Department of Health after widespread research highlighted the damage that was done to youngsters' health from second-hand smoke in cars.

However, police chiefs had signalled that forces would turn a blind eye to the offence.

While they have the power to stop drivers and issue on-the-spot fines, chief officers have indicated they will not apply the law "forcefully" and will focus instead on taking a "non-confrontational" approach.

The National Police Chiefs' Council said drivers would be "educated" rather than prosecuted, leaving some critics to wonder if the message will succeed in getting through to drivers.

Now figures obtained under the Freedom of Information Act have confirmed that police are choosing not to enforce the law, which was hailed as "a landmark in protecting children from second-hand smoke".

In the first seven months, just three police forces in England and Wales reported incidents that were all dealt with by verbal warnings, the BBC reported.

The forces that recorded warnings were the Metropolitan Police, which issued two, Dyfed-Powys Police, which issued four, and Devon and Cornwall Police, which gave one warning.

The data, from 42 English and Welsh police forces, showed no fines have been issued.

Nigel Rabbits, branch spokesman for Devon and Cornwall Police Federation, told the BBC: "It is poor legislation that hasn't been thought through and it's very difficult to enforce because you are talking about looking at a vehicle and trying to figure out what's going on inside.

"If you're looking for someone under the age of 18 that's difficult without stopping the vehicle and once the vehicle has been stopped getting the evidence for prosecution is extremely difficult."

Experts think up to three million children are exposed to smoke in cars, putting them at risk of serious conditions including asthma, bronchitis and infections of the chest and ear.

The introduction of the legislation followed similar changes in the law to make all work vehicles smoke-free and outlaws even those who smoke with their window wound down.

The Department of Health said many people smoking with children in the car were unaware of how harmful it could be.

"In changing the law we always said the measure of success would be in changes in attitude and behaviour, not number of enforcement actions," it said in a statement.

"As with other smoke-free legislation, we expect high levels of compliance with this change that will continue to grow."

29 June 2016

⇨ The above information is reprinted with kind permission from *The Telegraph*. Please visit www.telegraph.co.uk for further information.

The toxic truth behind smoking in cars with children

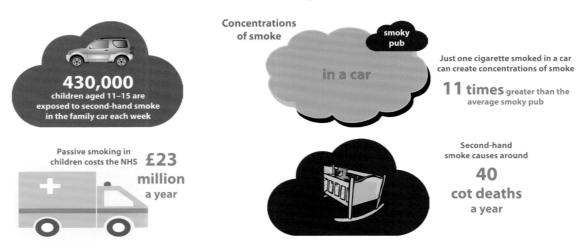

430,000 children aged 11–15 are exposed to second-hand smoke in the family car each week

Passive smoking in children costs the NHS **£23 million** a year

Concentrations of smoke

in a car

smoky pub

Just one cigarette smoked in a car can create concentrations of smoke **11 times** greater than the average smoky pub

Second-hand smoke causes around **40 cot deaths** a year

E-cigarettes are a gateway to real cigarettes for Britain's young

An article from The Conversation.

By Mark Conner, Professor, University of Leeds

THE CONVERSATION

Young people in Britain who use e-cigarettes (vape) are nearly four times more likely to start smoking cigarettes than their non-vaping peers, our latest study has found.

When e-cigarettes first entered the market a decade ago, they were considered to be as dangerous as cigarettes. But views have changed since then, and e-cigarettes are now widely believed to be a far safer option than smoking.

In 2015, Public Health England published a detailed review of the evidence around the safety of e-cigarettes and said, at best guess, they were 95% less toxic than conventional cigarettes.

But concerns remain because e-cigarettes usually contain the addictive ingredient of cigarettes: nicotine. While recognising the harm reduction impact of e-cigarettes, it is important to ask what role, if any, e-cigarettes play in encouraging non-smoking adolescents to try their first cigarette.

For a number of years, my colleagues and I have been tracking data from several thousand schoolchildren in England to assess the impact of various anti-smoking interventions. We set about trying to identify any associations between e-cigarette use and starting to smoke within a year.

We started by looking at those children, aged 14 and 15, who had not smoked. We asked them to fill out a questionnaire at the start of the survey, and then a year later. Of those who had tried an e-cigarette, just under 34% reported having a cigarette within a year compared with just under 9% who had not. In other words, there was an almost fourfold increased chance of starting to smoke among those young people who had used an e-cigarette. This is worrying because it is known that once someone starts to smoke, the chances that they will continue to smoke are high.

Would they have started smoking anyway?

Last year, researchers in the US published their findings on smoking among a group of teenagers (average age 17) in southern California. As with our study in England, they were surveyed at the start of the study and again 16 months later. The US researchers found that e-cigarette users had six times the risk of starting to smoke compared with their peers, who had not used an e-cigarette.

Perhaps these young people were going to smoke anyway, whether e-cigarettes existed or not? It is a question that gets to the heart of the risks that might be associated with e-cigarette use among the young.

We looked at those adolescents whose friends did or did not smoke, because having friends who smoke is a known risk factor for starting smoking. The data – which surprised us – suggested that e-cigarette use was a greater risk factor in starting to smoke in those without friends who smoked, compared with those with friends who smoked.

Using e-cigarettes meant they were five-and-a-half times more likely to start smoking in the group with no friends who smoked but only one-and-a-half times more likely to start smoking in the group with most or all friends who smoked.

Again, the picture in the US seems very similar to what we found in the UK. Researchers there found associations between e-cigarette use and starting to smoke among those young people who during the initial survey stated they had no intention of starting to smoke.

So what do the associations suggest is going on? The unanswered question is whether the young people who go on to smoke are simply experimenting or whether they are becoming regular smokers.

The long-term trend in the UK is for e-cigarette use to go up while smoking declines. Future research is now needed to disentangle these apparently contrary findings, and whether there is any link between the intensity of e-cigarette use among adolescents and cigarette use.

18 August 2017

⇨ The above information is reprinted with kind permission from *The Conversation*. Please visit www.theconversation.com for further information.

Smoking just one cigarette a day can seriously damage your health

Whether you have one a day or 20, the damage is still huge.

By Natasha Hinde

Smoking just one cigarette a day raises the risk of developing coronary heart disease and stroke far more than first thought, a new study suggests.

Researchers compared the effects of smoking a single cigarette to smoking 20 a day and found there wasn't a huge difference in the effects. In fact, smoking one a day only halved the risk of heart disease when compared to smoking 20.

Researchers said their findings have important consequences for many smokers and health professionals who believe that smoking just a few cigarettes carries little or no harm.

They warned smokers to stop smoking completely instead of cutting down.

Individual studies have reported that smoking only one to five cigarettes per day is associated with a higher than expected risk of heart disease.

To investigate this further, a team of researchers led by Professor Allan Hackshaw at the Cancer Institute at University College London analysed the results of 141 studies and estimated the relative risks for smoking one, five or 20 cigarettes per day.

If the risk for smoking 20 cigarettes per day is 100%, the expected risk for smoking one a day is around 5%. However for both genders, the actual risk turned out to be much higher:

⇨ Men who smoked one cigarette per day had 46% of the risk of heart disease associated with smoking 20 cigarettes per day.

⇨ Men who smoked one cigarette per day had 41% of the risk of stroke associated with smoking 20 cigarettes per day.

⇨ Women who smoked one cigarette per day had 31% of the risk of heart disease associated with smoking 20 cigarettes per day.

⇨ Women who smoked one cigarette per day had 34% of the risk of stroke associated with smoking 20 cigarettes per day.

⇨ Women's heart disease risk was more than doubled with one cigarette per day.

The study's authors wrote in *The BMJ*: "We have shown that a large proportion of the risk of coronary heart disease and stroke comes from smoking only a couple of cigarettes each day. This probably comes as a surprise to many people. But there are also biological mechanisms that help explain the unexpectedly high risk associated with a low level of smoking."

They acknowledged some study limitations, but said their paper is the first to combine results across many studies covering both coronary heart disease and stroke.

They hailed the findings as "a valuable reference that can be used to strengthen public health campaigns, and provide a strong health incentive for smokers to stop completely (particularly women)".

Cardiovascular disease, not cancer, is the greatest mortality risk for smoking,

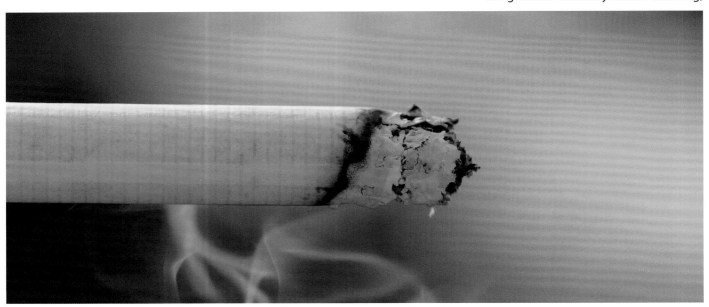

causing about 48% of smoking-related premature deaths.

The authors concluded: "No safe level of smoking exists for cardiovascular disease. Smokers should quit instead of cutting down, using appropriate cessation aids if needed, to significantly reduce their risk of these two common major disorders."

In a linked editorial, Kenneth Johnson, Adjunct Professor at the University of Ottawa, outlined the major public health implications of these results, and said "only complete cessation [quitting] is protective and should be emphasised by all prevention measures and policies".

The take home message for smokers is that "any exposure to cigarette smoke is too much," he added. "The message for regulators dealing with newly marketed 'reduced risk' products is that any suggestion of seriously reduced coronary heart disease and stroke from using these products is premature."

Deborah Arnott, chief executive of health charity ASH, said: "Many smokers think that they're not at risk if they only smoke one or two a day. This research shows that's just not true, particularly when it comes to heart disease and stroke.

"If you can't quit, get help. Smokers are up to four times as likely to succeed if they get help from their local stop smoking service or GP than if they try to quit unaided."

21 January 2018

⇨ The above information is reprinted with kind permission from The Huffington Post UK. Please visit www.huffingtonpost.co.uk for further information.

Electronic cigarettes could have a huge effect on public health THE CONVERSATION

An article from The Conversation.

By Marcus Munafo, Professor of Biological Psychology, University of Bristol

Tobacco still kills 6 million people around the world every year. Despite huge public health efforts to help people quit and prevent young people starting, smoking remains the single greatest cause of ill health and premature death. And even with restrictions on tobacco advertising and smoking in public places, many young people continue to take up smoking. The situation is even worse in poorer countries, where support to stop smoking is limited, and tobacco control policies weaker.

So in light of this, how should we view the increasing popularity of electronic cigarettes? The gadgets deliver a nicotine hit by heating a nicotine-containing propylene glycol (e-liquid) to create an aerosol (usually called 'vapour'), which is inhaled. Put simply, they deliver nicotine almost as effectively as a conventional cigarette, but without the vast majority of other chemicals present in tobacco smoke (either from the tobacco itself, or as a result of the burning process).

A whole culture is emerging around 'vaping'. Many devices offer a range of power settings, and a vast array of e-liquids is on offer, with varying nicotine contents and flavours. Enthusiasts often apply modifications to their devices, and engage in 'cloud chasing' – competing to produce the largest and most interesting clouds of vapour. And yes, young people are experimenting with e-cigarettes (in the same way that they have always experimented with pretty much everything), although at the moment there is no strong evidence this is leading to subsequent cigarette use, or even long-term e-cigarette use.

The rapid growth in use of e-cigarettes, especially among smokers trying to cut down or quit, has taken the public health community and the tobacco industry by surprise. Both are struggling to catch up. Health professionals are hurrying to carry out research to develop evidence-based guidelines and policies. Meanwhile, the tobacco industry is buying up e-cigarette companies and introducing its own products onto the market.

So how concerned should we be about this emerging and disruptive technology?

Should we encourage existing smokers to use e-cigarettes to help them stop smoking, even if this means they continue using nicotine long-term? In the United Kingdom there is some consensus that smokers should be encouraged to use e-cigarettes if they feel they might help, and the National Centre for Smoking Cessation and Training is supportive of their use. Part of the reason many vapers feel so passionately about the subject (and react strongly when they feel that vaping is being unfairly attacked) is that for the first time, through the use of e-cigarettes, they have felt able to take control of their nicotine

habit, stop smoking, and reassert some control over their health, without being medicalised in the process.

But a problem remains in the lack of information on the possible harm of e-cigarettes. This is unlikely to change any time soon, since the health effects of tobacco use can take several decades to emerge, and it's probable the same will be true for e-cigarettes. Nothing is entirely risk-free, but the vastly reduced number of chemicals present in e-cigarette vapour compared to tobacco smoke means we can be confident that vaping will be much, much less harmful than smoking.

Heartening evidence

As part of the investigation into the effects of e-cigarettes, we investigated how the cells found in the arteries of the heart, known as human coronary artery endothelial cells, responded when they were exposed to both e-cigarette vapour and conventional cigarette smoke. We found the cells showed a clear stress response from the cigarette smoke, but not from the electronic cigarette. This suggests tobacco smokers may be able to reduce immediate tobacco-related harm by switching from conventional cigarettes to e-cigarettes.

Many people find it difficult to function without their first caffeine hit of the day. But no one is seriously calling for coffee shops to be dismantled or regulated. Nicotine is addictive, but much less so on its own than in tobacco, where other chemicals enhance its effect. At the doses consumed by vapers the harm is likely to be very low (although we need to continue to research this), and many vapers actually gradually move to zero nicotine content e-liquids, even while continuing to vape.

Of course, we may end up with a large population of long-term nicotine users who use e-cigarettes to deliver nicotine rather than cigarettes, but all of the evidence at the moment suggests that this population will almost entirely comprise ex-smokers. This would produce a vast public health gain.

We must be careful not to restrict smokers' access to e-cigarettes, or over-state the potential harm of their use, if this will put people off making the transition from smoking to vaping. To do so would deny us one of the greatest public health improving opportunities of the last 50 years.

20 June 2016

⇨ The above information is reprinted with kind permission from *The Conversation*. Please visit www. theconversation.com for further information.

What are the health risks of smoking?

Smoking is one of the biggest causes of death and illness in the UK.

Every year around 100,000 people in the UK die from smoking, with many more living with debilitating smoking-related illnesses.

Smoking increases your risk of developing more than 50 serious health conditions. Some may be fatal and others can cause irreversible long-term damage to your health.

You can become ill:

⇨ if you smoke yourself

⇨ through other people's smoke (passive smoking).

Smoking health risks

Smoking causes about 90% of lung cancers. It also causes cancer in many other parts of the body, including the:

⇨ mouth

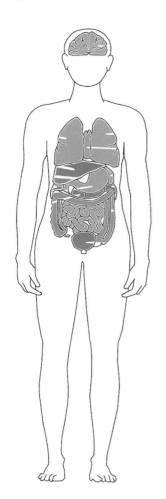

⇨ lips

⇨ throat

⇨ voice box (larynx)

⇨ oesophagus (the tube between your mouth and stomach)

⇨ bladder

⇨ kidney

⇨ liver

⇨ stomach

⇨ pancreas.

Smoking damages your heart and your blood circulation, increasing your risk of developing conditions such as:

⇨ coronary heart disease

⇨ heart attack

⇨ stroke

⇨ peripheral vascular disease (damaged blood vessels)

⇨ cerebrovascular disease (damaged arteries that supply blood to your brain)

Smoking also damages your lungs, leading to conditions such as:

⇨ chronic obstructive pulmonary disease (COPD), which incorporates bronchitis and emphysema

⇨ pneumonia.

Smoking can also worsen or prolong the symptoms of respiratory conditions such as asthma, or respiratory tract infections such as the common cold.

In men, smoking can cause impotence because it limits the blood supply to the penis. It can also reduce the fertility of both men and women.

Health risks of passive smoking

Second-hand smoke comes from the tip of a lit cigarette and the smoke that the smoker breathes out.

Breathing in second-hand smoke – also known as passive smoking – increases your risk of getting the same health conditions as smokers. For example, breathing in second-hand smoke increases a non-smoker's risk of developing lung cancer by about a quarter.

Babies and children are particularly vulnerable to the effects of second-hand smoke. A child who is exposed to passive smoke is at increased risk of developing chest infections, meningitis, a persistent cough and, if they have asthma, their symptoms will get worse. They're also at increased risk of cot death and an ear infection called glue ear.

Health risks of smoking during pregnancy

If you smoke when you're pregnant, you put your unborn baby's health at risk, as well as your own. Smoking during pregnancy increases the risk of complications such as:

⇨ miscarriage

⇨ premature (early) birth

⇨ a low birth weight baby

⇨ stillbirth.

Getting help

Your GP can give you information and advice on quitting smoking. You can also call:

⇨ the NHS Smokefree helpline on 0300 123 1044.

28 November 2015

⇨ The above information is reprinted with kind permission from NHS Choices. Please visit www.nhs.uk for further information.

© NHS Choices 2018

Towards a smokefree generation

An extract from A Tobacco Control Plan for England.

Our national ambitions

Our vision is to create a smokefree generation. We will have achieved this when smoking prevalence is at 5% or below. To deliver this, the Government sets out the following national ambitions which will help focus tobacco control across the whole system:

1. The first smokefree generation

People should be supported not to start smoking, so we aim, by the end of 2022 to:

⇨ Reduce the prevalence of 15-year-olds who regularly smoke from 8% to 3% or less.

⇨ Reduce smoking prevalence amongst adults in England from 15.5% to 12% or less.

⇨ Reduce the inequality gap in smoking prevalence between those in routine and manual occupations and the general population.

To do this we need all public services to work together, leading the way in helping people to stop smoking.

After 2022, we will continue to reduce smoking prevalence further, on our way to a smokefree generation.

2. A smokefree pregnancy for all

Every child deserves the best start in life, so we aim, by the end of 2022 to:

⇨ Reduce the prevalence of smoking in pregnancy from 10.7% to 6% or less.

3. Parity of esteem for those with mental health conditions

People with mental ill health should be given equal priority to those with physical ill health, so we aim to:

⇨ Improve data collected on smoking and mental health to help us to support people with mental health conditions to quit smoking.

⇨ Make all mental health inpatient services sites smokefree by 2018.

4. Backing evidence based innovations to support quitting

We are committed to evidence-based policy making, so we aim to:

⇨ Help people to quit smoking by permitting innovative technologies that minimise the risk of harm.

⇨ Maximise the availability of safer alternatives to smoking.

Action

To achieve these ambitions we have developed a new tobacco control plan, targeted around four main themes, with a range of actions for each. These actions include:

1. Prevention first

To achieve a smokefree generation we will:

⇨ Ensure the effective operation of legislation such as proxy purchasing and standardised packaging designed to reduce the uptake of smoking by young people.

⇨ Support pregnant smokers to quit. NICE has produced guidance on how pregnant smokers can be helped to quit. Public Health England and NHS England will work together on the implementation of this guidance.

2. Supporting smokers to quit

To achieve a smokefree generation we will:

⇨ Provide access to training for all health professionals on how to help patients – especially patients in mental health services – to quit smoking.

⇨ NHS Trusts will encourage smokers using, visiting and working in the NHS to quit, with the goal of creating a smokefree NHS by 2020 through the 5 Year Forward View mandate.

3. Eliminating variations in smoking rates

To reduce the regional and socio-economic variations in smoking rates, we need to achieve system-wide change and target our actions at the right groups so we will:

⇨ Promote links to 'stop smoking' services across the health and care system and full implementation of all relevant NICE guidelines by 2022.

⇨ Support local councils to help people to quit by working with Directors of Public Health to identify local solutions, particularly where prevalence remains high.

4. Effective enforcement

To reduce the demand for tobacco and continue to develop an environment that protects young people and others from the harms of smoking we will:

⇨ Maintain high duty rates for tobacco products to make tobacco less affordable.

⇨ Ensure that sanctions in current legislation are effective and fit for purpose, using lessons from

HMRC's work on sanctions to stop illicit tobacco.

The evidence – and the costs

Where we are now

Smoking remains the single largest cause of preventable deaths and one of the largest causes of health inequalities in England. There are still 7.3 million adult smokers and more than 200 people a day die from smoking-related illness which could have been prevented.

During the period covered by the last tobacco control plan (2011–15), prevalence across all target groups dropped. This is a huge achievement.

But these headline numbers disguise the fact that smoking and its associated harms continue to fall hardest on some of the poorest and most vulnerable people in our society. The difference in life expectancy between the poorest and the richest can be as much as nine years. Smoking accounts for approximately half of this difference. This is an injustice which must be addressed.

As well as dying prematurely, smokers also suffer many years in poor health. Many of the conditions caused by smoking are chronic illnesses which can be debilitating for the sufferer and make it difficult to carry out day-to-day tasks and engage with society and the economy. Smokers proportionately are less likely to be in work.

From 2012 to 2015 smoking-related mortality was around 50% greater in the north-east compared to the south-west. But smoking blights poorer communities across the country. The local authority with the highest rate of smoking is Hastings, which has a prevalence of 26% among adults.

The cost of smoking to society

Smoking causes around 79,000 preventable deaths in England and is estimated to cost our economy in excess of £11 billion per year. Of this cost:

£2.5 billion fell to the NHS

In 2015/16, there were approximately 474,000 smoking-related hospital admissions with smokers also seeing their GP 35% more than non-smokers. These costs add a great burden to a system already dealing with growing demand.

£5.3 billion fell to employers

Smokers are, on average, absent from work 2.7 days more per year compared to ex- and non-smokers. In 2014 this is estimated to have led to a loss of economic output of around £1.7 billion. Smoking breaks also result in lost output for employers estimated at around £3.6 billion a year.

£4.1 billion fell to wider society

Smoking results in the death or absence of people who would otherwise be working and contributing to the economy. Accounting for potential lifetime earnings, it is estimated that smoking-attributable deaths in 2014 resulted in a total output loss of around £3.1 billion. Unemployment and economic inactivity due to smoking-attributable ill health also results in lost output to the economy, estimated at around £1.0 billion per year.

The further costs of tobacco

Smoking-related ill health also leads to increased costs for the adult social care system. One study estimates that local councils face a demand pressure of £760 million a year on domiciliary (home) care services, as a result of smoking-related health conditions.

The true cost of tobacco use is likely to be higher than the figures provided here, with evidence now showing that smoking causes a greater range of diseases and death than accounted for in these costs. Every year, additional costs are also incurred from smoking related fires and tobacco litter, as well as the wider costs associated with illicit tobacco and organised crime.

Prevention First

A smokefree generation

Work to eliminate smoking among under-18s and achieve the first smokefree generation.

Smoking remains an addiction which is largely taken up in childhood, with the majority of smokers starting as teenagers. 77% of smokers aged 16 to 24 in 2014 began smoking before the age of 18. As a result many young people become addicted before they fully understand the health risks associated with smoking.

Discouraging young people from smoking remains a priority, which is why we want to reduce the prevalence of 15-year-olds who regularly smoke to 3% or less by the end of 2022.

However, 32% of smokers (current and ex-smokers) aged 16–24 started when they were 16 or 17. Therefore as smoking prevalence in 15-year-olds continues to decline, we will also review the data on 16- and 17-year-olds to help inform our understanding of the trends in smoking amongst young people.

One of the most effective ways to reduce the number of young people smoking is to reduce the number of adults who smoke. We know that children are heavily influenced by adult role models who smoke: in 2014, 82% of pupils who regularly smoked reported having a family member who smoked. Continuing to encourage adult smokers to quit must therefore remain an important part of reducing prevalence amongst the young, and achieving a smokefree generation.

Research shows that in 2014, 46% of pupils aged 11 to 15 who were current (regular and occasional) smokers usually bought their cigarettes in shops, despite the law which prohibits the sale of cigarettes to those under the age of 18. Breaking age of sale laws puts young people at risk and it is clear that we must more effectively enforce laws designed to protect young people.

July 2017

⇨ The above extract is reprinted with kind permission from GOV. UK. Please visit www.assets. publishing.service.gov.uk for further information.

Stopping smoking is good for your mental health

We all know that stopping smoking improves your physical health.

But it's also proven to boost your mental health and well-being: it can improve mood and help relieve stress, anxiety and depression.

Smoking, anxiety and mood

Most smokers say they want to stop, but some continue because smoking seems to relieve stress and anxiety.

But it's a complete myth that smoking helps you relax. Smoking actually increases anxiety and tension.

Smokers are also more likely than non-smokers to develop depression or anxiety disorder over time.

Why it feels like smoking helps us relax

Smoking cigarettes interferes with certain chemicals in the brain.

When smokers haven't had a cigarette for a while, the craving for another one makes them feel irritable and anxious.

These feelings can be temporarily relieved when they light up a cigarette. So smokers associate the improved mood with smoking.

In fact, it's the effects of smoking itself that's likely to have caused the anxiety in the first place.

Cutting out smoking does improve mood and reduces anxiety.

The mental health benefits of quitting smoking

When people stop smoking, studies show:

⇨ anxiety, depression and stress levels are lower

⇨ quality of life and positive mood improve

⇨ the dosage of some medicines used to treat mental health problems can be reduced

Smokers with mental health problems

People with mental health problems, including anxiety, depression or schizophrenia:

⇨ are much more likely to smoke than the general population

⇨ tend to smoke more heavily

⇨ die on average ten to 20 years earlier than those who don't experience mental health problems – smoking plays a major role in this difference in life expectancy

⇨ need higher doses of some antipsychotic medicines and antidepressants because smoking interferes with the way these medicines work.

Stopping smoking can be as effective as antidepressants

People with mental health problems are likely to feel much calmer and more positive, and have a better quality of life, after giving up smoking.

Evidence suggests the beneficial effect of stopping smoking on symptoms of anxiety and depression can equal that of taking antidepressants.

Five tips to stop smoking

If you want to stop smoking, contact your local stop smoking service, which provides the best chance of stopping completely and forever.

Here are four ways to boost your chances of stopping smoking for good:

⇨ Use stop smoking aids like nicotine replacement therapy (NRT) or e-cigarettes.

⇨ See a stop smoking expert. It's free and will increase your chances of quitting for good.

You can talk about which stop smoking aids will work best for you, and they can provide additional support such as advice on managing cravings. They can also talk to you about the two stop smoking medicines available on prescription: Varenicline (Champix) and Bupropion (Zyban).

⇨ If you're not as successful as you want to be, you'll still have learnt something to help you next time. The more comfortable you are using the support available, the better prepared you'll be for stopping completely next time.

⇨ If you take antipsychotic medicines or antidepressants, it's important you talk to your GP or psychiatrist before you stop smoking – the dosage of these medicines may need to be monitored and the amount you need to take could be reduced.

25 January 2018

⇨ The above information is reprinted with kind permission from NHS Choices. Please visit www.nhs.uk for further information.

Eight things that have changed since the smoking ban ten years ago

An article from The Conversation.

THE CONVERSATION

By Andrew Russell, Associate Professor and Fellow of the Wolfson Research Institute for Health and Wellbeing, Durham University

It's hard to think back to what English pubs and clubs were like before the law about smokefree public places came into force ten years ago. Do you remember the dense fog, the smell of tobacco smoke on your clothes and hair after a night out, and the ashtrays loaded with cigarette butts?

The change in law has been described as:

⇨ The most important piece of public health legislation for a generation.

Of course, bringing it in had its challenges. Various options were proposed, including a plan to exempt private clubs and pubs that didn't serve food – so-called 'wet pubs' – but in some parts of England this would have excluded over half of all licensed premises.

Eventually, this proposal was quashed, mainly because of public health concerns. People with jobs forcing them to remain in smoky environments often had no choice but to do so – and why should they be subject to the health risks of second-hand smoke?

But apart from making public places more pleasant and healthier to be in, the new law also had some unexpected results.

1. More people have given up smoking

There was a spike in people deciding to stop smoking as a result of the ban. Everyone knew the health risks of smoking – the ban simply cut out many of the places where people might have wanted to light up.

Ever since the law came into force, smoking rates have gone down year-on-year. And increasingly, young people in particular seem to be going off the idea. The number of children under 16 who regularly smoke has halved to 3% since 2007 – the lowest figure on record.

2. Fewer people hospitalised

Figures also soon showed a significant decline in hospital admissions for heart attacks, asthma and lung infections. In the year following the law, there were 2.4% fewer heart attack cases recorded in Accident and Emergency departments than the year before. This might not sound very much, but that is 1,200 fewer cases in the country as a whole.

These figures are even more dramatic if you bear in mind that many workplaces had already gone smokefree before the law came into effect. This makes the fact we can see a distinct drop before and after the ban came into place even more remarkable.

3. Goodbye glossy packs

The success of the ban also gave people the courage to tackle other smoking-related issues that might once have seemed impossible to address – such as plain packaging and other forms of advertising at the point of sale.

Figures from Australia – which imposed plain packaging three years before the UK – found that restricting the colour, size and font on cigarette packets led to a noticeable drop in the number of people smoking.

Similar projections were made for the UK, with scientists claiming plain packets could encourage more than 300,000 Britons to quit smoking for good.

4. Increased awareness of passive smoking

The smokefree law also made people more aware of the dangers of second-hand smoke everywhere, including in their own homes. This is a step in the right direction for people with long-term lung conditions – as the Life of Breath project at Durham and Bristol universities shows how sensitive to air quality these people are. For them a smoke-filled environment is a nightmare.

5. No more smoking at stations

Some companies went further than required by the new law. The Association of Train Operator Companies and Network Rail, decided to make all station premises smokefree. Perhaps they were remembering the fire at Kings Cross underground station in 1987. It killed 31 and was blamed on a lit match thrown away by a smoker exiting the station.

6. Drop in teen smokers

Vending machines, where young people could often obtain their cigs out of the watchful eye of adults, are also a thing of the past. And it is now illegal to buy cigarettes if you are under 18. This was previously set at the age of 16 before 2007.

Taxes on tobacco products have also continued to rise, making it even more difficult for young people with less money in their pocket.

7. Smoking banned in cars with kids

Smoking in private cars where children are present is now banned. This is important because children suffer more from second-hand smoke than adults, as their airways are smaller and they breathe faster.

And yet smoking in pregnancy – with the risks this carries for mother and baby – are still high in some parts of Britain. And surprisingly, given the ease with which tobacco addiction can be managed these days, smoking is still allowed in some NHS grounds.

8. E-cigs have arrived

E-cigarettes have muddied the waters of tobacco control, because although they are without doubt safer than cigarettes, some people firmly believe they too should be part of the smokefree laws.

Whatever your view on that score, support for smoke free places is higher now than it was when the law first came in. In other words, there are very few people – both smokers and non-smokers – who would like to return to those foggy days of smoke-filled clubs and bars.

28 June 2017

⇨ The above information is reprinted with kind permission from *The Conversation*. Please visit www. theconversation.com for further information.

NHS hospitals should sell e-cigarettes, say government agency

Smoking shelters should become "vaping lounges" for less risky e-cigarette use, NHS bosses said.

By Alex Matthews-King, Health Correspondent

Hospitals should stock e-cigarettes for sale to patients and permit "vaping" in private rooms as part of the NHS "smokefree" efforts, according to health chiefs.

The call comes from Public Health England, as part of an evidence update on the safety of tobacco alternatives which it says should be used more widely as quitting aids.

Meanwhile, government officials should help manufacturers license e-cigarettes as medical quitting aids.

Such a move would allow GPs to prescribe the devices to their patients who are trying to stop smoking.

In the independent review, which updates 2015 guidance, experts concluded that vaping only poses a small fraction of the risks of smoking and could be particularly helpful in mental health hospitals.

These patients are often on a long-term stay, and have high levels of smoking and tobacco-related harm which could be mitigated by promoting vaping.

E-cigarettes could be contributing to 20,000 new quits each year, they estimated.

But the number of people using the products has "plateaued" and now stands at just under three million people in the UK, according to the review, which was conducted by experts from King's College London and the UK Centre for Tobacco and Alcohol Studies, the University of Stirling and Cancer Research UK.

One reason behind the stall in uptake could be misconceptions about the levels of harm linked to the devices.

Researchers found that thousands of smokers "incorrectly" believe that vaping is as harmful as smoking and two in five smokers had not even tried an e-cigarette.

In a linked editorial, published in *The Lancet*, experts from PHE said: "Although not without risk, the overall risk of harm is estimated at less than 5% of that from smoking tobacco; the risk of cancer has been calculated to be less than 1%."

PHE officials also warned about the risks of tobacco industry efforts to promote "heat not burn" tobacco products as a safer alternatives to regular cigarettes.

It warns that while these combustion-free alternatives currently appear to have some reduced risk, the majority of the research has been conducted in the tobacco industry.

Following the review, PHE has made a number of recommendations about e-cigarettes, including a call for the Medicines and Healthcare Products Regulatory Agency to support manufacturers to license the products as medical quit aids so they can be made available on the NHS; encouraging any smoker to switch to using e-cigarettes, and calling on NHS trusts to be "truly smoke free", and as part of this, ensuring e-cigarettes are for sale in hospital shops.

Martin Dockrell, tobacco control lead for PHE, said: "We are saying no smoking anywhere on the grounds [of hospitals], no smoking in the smoking shelter – that shelter becomes a vaping shelter.

"There are two parts to being a smoke-free hospital, one is not allowing smoking on the premises, the other is helping every smoker to quit.

"Some hospitals will decide, especially with their longer-term patients or patients who don't have a choice whether they are there or not, where it will be appropriate to have spaces indoors to have spaces where vaping is permitted.

"The strongest case for that is psychiatric hospitals because [these patients] have got the highest prevalence of smoking and the highest levels of smoking-related harm.

"Single occupancy rooms are quite common in mental health trusts so that makes it very easy for people to vape in a single occupancy room without any annoyance to anybody else."

On acute hospitals he added: "It is going to be for each hospital to make their own policy but yes, we would certainly encourage them to make at least some single occupancy rooms where people can vape. Of course smoking is prohibited everywhere."

When asked about indoor communal rooms for vaping, Mr Dockrell said: "There is no reason why a hospital shouldn't designate some indoor areas where patients and visitors can vape."

Professor John Newton, director for health improvement at PHE, said: "Our new review reinforces the finding that vaping is a fraction of the risk of smoking, at least 95% less harmful, and of negligible risk to bystanders.

"Yet over half of smokers either falsely believe that vaping is as harmful as smoking or just don't know.

"It would be tragic if thousands of smokers who could quit with the help of an e-cigarette are being put off due to false fears about their safety."

Ann McNeill, lead author and professor of tobacco addiction at King's College London, said: "It's of great concern that smokers still have such a poor understanding about what causes the harm from smoking.

"People smoke for the nicotine, but contrary to what the vast majority believe, nicotine causes little if any of the harm.

However pro-smoking groups argued PHE's endorsement could be enough to keep people smoking tobacco, by making e-cigarettes "just another smoking cessation aid".

"If that happens they will almost certainly lose their appeal to independent-minded smokers who don't want the state dictating their behaviour," said Simon Clark, director of the smokers' group Forest.

6 February 2018

⇨ The above information is reprinted with kind permission from *The Independent*. Please visit www.independent.co.uk for further information.

ASH Wales welcomes new laws protecting children from smoking

New laws to protect children and young people from the harms of tobacco have been hailed as a major public health achievement by tobacco control campaign group ASH Wales.

The Public Health (Wales) Bill successfully passed in the Senedd (Tuesday, 16 May) following a final vote by Assembly Members.

The new laws will restrict smoking in children's playgrounds, school grounds and hospital sites and pave the way for a retail register of all tobacco sellers. The legislation follows a campaign by ASH Wales which persuaded every local authority in Wales to implement voluntary smoking bans in their children's playgrounds and has seen 11 councils ban smoking at the gates of their primary schools.

Research shows young people are highly influenced by others smoking around them – those with a parent who smokes are 70% more likely to take up the habit. Smokefree areas also protect from second-hand smoke whilst 'denormalising' the deadly habit. Almost half of long-term smokers begin smoking before leaving high school and among children who try smoking around a third become regular smokers within three years.

Support for banning smoking at communal outdoor spaces such as these – especially those specifically created for children – remains high. A recent YouGov poll (2017) showed:

⇨ 71% agree smoking should be banned in hospital grounds

⇨ 61% agree with banning smoking in recreational spaces such as parks and beaches

⇨ An overwhelming 83% think smoking should be banned at children's playgrounds, including 56% of smokers.

One of the most powerful control measures outlined in the Bill is the creation of a national register of retailers of tobacco products. This will make it easier for retailers to be identified and monitored – helping to tackle the problem of illegal sales of tobacco to underage young people in Wales.

Suzanne Cass, Chief Executive ASH Wales Cymru, said: "This is a major public health achievement and it is absolutely fantastic news that Wales' next generation have the chance to grow up in a society where they can get an education, play and meet their friends in smokefree, clean environments.

"Smoking is an addiction of childhood with a classroom full of children taking up smoking every day in Wales. It is essential tobacco control measures tackle the issue of young people smoking or seeing this adult choice as a normal, everyday activity. It is essential we set positive examples wherever we can.

"The retail register will give enforcement agencies a clear idea of where tobacco is being sold and the increased restrictions will help drive down the sale of illegal tobacco. Illegal tobacco is sold at pocket money prices by sellers who don't care about age restrictions, therefore making tobacco more accessible to young people."

The Bill has seen various health organisations such as Cancer Research UK, British Heart Foundation and ASH Wales work tirelessly over the past few years to provide strong evidence to support the tobacco control aspects which will become law following Royal Assent.

16 May 2017

⇨ The above information is reprinted with kind permission from ASH Wales. Please visit www.ashwales. org.uk for futher information.

Plain cigarette packaging could drive 300,000 Britons to quit smoking

Review by research organisation Cochrane suggests impact of UK's ban on branded packs could echo results seen in Australia.

By Sarah Bosely, Health Editor

Plain cigarette cartons featuring large, graphic health warnings could persuade 300,000 people in the UK to quit smoking if the measure has the effect it had in Australia, scientists say.

Standardised cigarette packaging will be compulsory in the UK from 20 May. A new review from the independent health research organisation Cochrane on the impact of plain packaging around the world has found that it does affect the behaviour of smokers.

In the UK, the tobacco industry has become increasingly innovative in the design of cigarette packets as other controls on sales and advertising have taken hold, according to Ann McNeill, Professor of Tobacco Addiction at King's College London. "The tobacco industry has been focusing its efforts on the tobacco packs," she said.

Among those that will be banned are vibrant pink packets, targeted at young women, and gimmicky cartons that slide rather than flip open. The rules that come into force next month require all packs to look alike, with graphic health warnings across 65% of their surface.

The Cochrane reviewers found 51 studies that looked at standardised packaging and its impact on smokers, but only one country had implemented the rule fully at the time. Australia brought in plain packs in 2012.

Analysing the evidence from Australia, the team found a reduction in smoking of 0.5% up to one year after the policy was introduced. According to the Australian Government, that translates to 100,000 people no longer smoking. The decline was attributable specifically to plain packaging, after taking into account the continuing drop in the numbers of smokers caused by other tobacco control measures.

Dr Jamie Hartmann-Boyce of the Cochrane tobacco addiction group at Oxford University's Nuffield Department of Primary Care Health Sciences said: "We are not able to say for sure what the impact would be in the UK, but if the same magnitude of decrease was seen in the UK as was observed in Australia, this would translate to roughly 300,000 fewer smokers following the implementation of standardised packaging."

The review found signs that more people were trying to quit smoking as a result of plain cartons, rising from 20.2% before to 26.6% after introduction. There was also evidence that standardised packs were less attractive to those who did not smoke, making it less likely that they would start.

However, the researchers say variations in the way countries are introducing standardised packs may affect the outcomes. Some allow different colours, slightly different carton shapes and the use of descriptive words such as 'gold' or 'smooth'.

Cancer Research UK backs plain packaging. "Smoking kills 100,000 people in the UK every year, so we support

any effective measure which can help reduce this devastating impact. The evidence shows that standardised packaging works and helps to reduce smoking rates," said George Butterworth, the charity's tobacco policy manager.

"It's too soon to see the impact in the UK, as the new legislation will only be fully implemented in May, but we hope to see similar positive results as the UK strives towards a day when no child smokes tobacco. Cancer Research UK is continuing to evaluate the impact of standardised packaging in the UK and will share the lessons with other countries who are considering introducing them."

Simon Clark, director of the smokers' group Forest, said the idea that plain packaging would have an impact on the number of smokers in the UK was based on "hope and anecdotal evidence".

"Since plain packaging was introduced in Australia, smoking rates have fallen, but only in line with historical trends," he said. "It's grasping at straws to credit plain packaging with the continued reduction in smoking rates, because the most significant anti-smoking measure in recent years in Australia has been a massive increase in tobacco taxation. Like graphic health warnings, the novelty of plain packaging quickly wears off."

27 April 2017

⇨ The above information is reprinted with kind permission from *The Guardian*. Please visit www.theguardian.com for further information.

Death of the cigarette on the horizon as tobacco giant invests in new 'safer' smoking devices

By Joe Shute

At the gates of the Papastratos tobacco factory, a bevy of glamorous hostesses dressed in identical black and wielding clipboards usher guests through. A helicopter whirs overhead while G4S security guards line the hill which winds down towards Athens in the distance.

Inside a cavernous marquee filled with politicians and captains of industry, André Calantzopoulos, chief executive of tobacco giant Philip Morris International (PMI) is preparing to unveil the future. "This revelation will change all that we know about smoking," he announces to the expectant crowd.

The revelation in question is a small plastic capsule into which specially-designed tobacco sticks are inserted and heated to 35° C allowing users to take puffs. In theory (according to PMI's own research) this reduces the risks of smoking by up to 95 per cent. What quite this means for people's health in the long run, however, remains a point of contention.

Big tobacco is gambling big on the rise in popularity of these devices, known as IQOS (I quit ordinary smoking). At the Papastratos factory last week PMI announced it would become the second of its tobacco factories to cease all production of ordinary cigarettes and instead churn out only the IQOS tobacco sticks, known as HEETS. Since 2008 the company has spent more than $4.5 billion in scientific research, production and commercial development of IQOS and related products.

Chances are you will never have seen an IQOS. As a tobacco product, PMI is banned from advertising it, hence why the company is keen to invite journalists through its factory gates. At present there are several IQOS stores selling the devices in Britain, all in London's trendier districts.

As with their counterparts in Athens the outlets are designed more like the Apple Store or a Nespresso outlet than a traditional tobacconist. The walls are bleached wood and potential customers are encouraged to "create your own IQOS experience" with a range of brightly coloured accessories. In the UK the cost of a starter pack (containing ten packs of HEETS tobacco sticks) is £121.50. It is difficult not to be left with the impression that the shops are designed to position IQOS as a trendy lifestyle brand – akin to having the latest smartphone.

The Athens branch is on a prestige stretch of high street sandwiched between shops selling Rolex and Bulgari watches and staffed by young trendy millennial sporting beards and asymmetric fringes.

They sit on sofas in earnest discussion with would-be customers who are a mix of 20-somethings and older smokers desperate to cut down. Tobacco consumption is falling in Greece but in the latest survey conducted last year 27.1 per cent of the population still admitted they were either regular or casual smokers.

By the end of 2018, according to staff at the factory, the aim is to produce 20 billion of the tobacco sticks a year. PMI – and the other big tobacco firms investing in similar technologies – insist this is all for the common good. But can the company that once sold us Marlboro Man really now be putting public health over profit?

According to Calantzopoulos, who joined the firm in 1985 and was appointed CEO in 2013, PMI and its stablemates are deserving of the chance to rehabilitate their reputations. "This rhetoric goes back to the Seventies and Eighties," he says.

"I think the world has changed in 40 years and companies do change as well."

"I don't ask people to trust," he adds. "I ask people to judge on facts and evaluate scientific assessment of this product."

So what are the health implications of a product an estimated five million people worldwide are already using?

Earlier this month, Public Health England (PHE) published its key findings on so-called heated tobacco products: IQOS, Glo, produced by British American Tobacco, and Ploom TECH by Japan Tobacco International. The devices are different to e-cigarettes as they still rely on using tobacco and therefore in theory allow the big companies a greater share of the profits.

The PHE study found compared to cigarettes the products were "likely to expose users and bystanders to lower levels of particulate matter and harmful and potentially harmful compounds", but the extent of the reduction varied between studies. It also admitted a dearth of independent research on the health impact – out of 20 studies included in its review, 12 were funded by tobacco manufacturing companies themselves.

In December the committee on toxicity (an advisory panel to the Government) released its own independent findings into the heated tobacco products. The committee admitted the devices produce "a number of compounds of concern", including some that can cause cancer. It also expressed concern young non-smokers might start using the products and that they could become a gateway to people smoking cigarettes.

Alan Boobis, Professor of Toxicology at Imperial College London who is chair of the committee, says while they discovered heated tobacco products reduce known toxic constituents of cigarettes by between 50 to 90 per cent, any reduction in the medium- to long-term health impact of smoking cannot be stated for certain because of the dearth of available independent evidence.

Professor Boobis says his committee is currently also researching the impact of e-cigarettes and have provisionally concluded they are preferable to heated tobacco from a health perspective. "The reality is big tobacco has clearly recognised the future of long-term cigarettes is very poor and they are trying to develop strategies to sell what they grow," he says.

"We have emphasised the advertising has to be responsible. They should not be targeted to under-age individuals, rather those who are current smokers and desperately trying to give up but cannot. They should not be trying to sell them to naive users."

Among those hoping IQOS can cure her habit is Marianna Mattheou, 51, who has been a smoker for more than 30 years and has a 30-a-day habit. She has been smoking IQOS for a month at the behest of her 14-year-old son but admits the devices have been leaving her with a sore throat. "I don't trust them 100 per cent," she says.

Alexandros Chatzopoulos is a manager of regulatory affairs at the Greek affiliate of PMI. He says the IQOS stores are steadfast in their refusal to sell the products to non-smokers and anybody aged under 18.

"We don't sell to non-smokers," he says.

Back in London I decide to put this claim to the test. I wander into the High Street Kensington IQOS store one lunchtime and tell the 20-something assistant who approaches me the truth – that I am an ex-smoker interested in the product.

She reiterates the rule that they do not sell to non-smokers but still leads me on

a tour of the shop, inviting me to touch the oversized heating blade on the wall to feel the warmth. At one point she grows suspicious of my questions and asks if I work for PMI, who apparently perform spot-checks to ensure staff follow proper procedures. At the end I am offered a brochure and told if I recommend the device to friends they will receive a discount.

I am left with the uneasy feeling that the new wave of smoking devices are creating regulatory grey areas – and these are the gaps in which tobacco giants are used to winning big.

30 March 2018

⇨ The above information is reprinted with kind permission from *The Telegraph*. Please visit www.telegraph.co.uk for further information.

Evidence review of e-cigarettes and heated tobacco products 2018: Executive summary

An extract from a report commissioned by Public Health England.

McNeill A, Brose LS, Calder R, Bauld L and Robson D (2018). Evidence review of e-cigarettes and heated tobacco products 2018

Heated tobacco products

Key findings

In mid-2017, heated tobacco products were commercially available in 27 countries and further country launches were planned. Three tobacco manufacturers were promoting heated tobacco products: 'IQOS' was promoted by Philip Morris International, 'glo' by British American Tobacco and 'Ploom TECH' by Japan Tobacco International.

Out of 20 studies that were included in this review, 12 were funded by manufacturing companies so there is a lack of independent research.

There is a variety of heated tobacco products, including some that deliver via both vapour and combustion.

Most studies published at the time of the search for this review evaluated IQOS, none evaluated glo or Ploom TECH. An updated version of the review including later publications is in preparation to be published separately.

In Great Britain, in 2017, awareness and even use of heated tobacco products were very rare.

Nicotine in mainstream aerosol from heated tobacco products reached 70%–84% of the nicotine detected in smoke from reference cigarettes.

The tested heated tobacco products delivered more nicotine in aerosol than a cigalike e-cigarette and less nicotine than a tank style e-cigarette.

Pharmacokinetics and delivery of nicotine after single use of a heated tobacco product were generally comparable with smoking a cigarette. However, studies that compared ad libitum use of heated tobacco products with smoking cigarettes consistently reported lower nicotine levels in heated tobacco product users compared with smokers.

Probably to compensate, smokers who were switched to using heated tobacco products adjusted their puffing behaviour.

Heated tobacco product use reduced urges to smoke, but smokers consistently reported heated tobacco product use to be less rewarding compared with smoking a cigarette.

Compared with cigarette smoke, heated tobacco products are likely to expose users and bystanders to lower levels of particulate matter and harmful and potentially harmful compounds. The extent of the reduction found varies between studies.

The limited evidence on environmental emissions from use of heated tobacco products suggests that harmful exposure from heated tobacco products is higher than from e-cigarettes, but further evidence is needed to be able to compare products.

Japan, where e-cigarettes are not available, has the most diverse heated tobacco product market with three tobacco manufacturers participating. Past 30-day use for the most frequently used product increased from 0.3% in 2015 to 3.7% in 2017, suggesting rapid penetration of heated tobacco products.

Implications

Research

There is a need for more research that is independent of commercial interests.

Different types of heated tobacco products will have different characteristics and effects, presenting a challenge for research.

Research is needed on relative risks of heated tobacco products to users and those around them compared with cigarettes and e-cigarettes.

Evidence is needed on appeal of heated tobacco products to smokers and non-smokers, particularly among youth.

Effects on smoking need to be researched, this includes whether they replace or complement cigarettes. Due to co-branding of some products with cigarettes and the more similar sensory profile, findings may be different than for e-cigarettes.

Future studies, whether funded by manufacturers or independently, should ensure conduct of studies in line with established guidelines such as definitions of abstinence from smoking, using intention-to-treat analysis and registering trial protocols prior to the start of participant recruitment.

The appropriateness of different methods for measuring emissions and their translation from cigarettes to heated tobacco products should be evaluated to be able to recommend a gold standard.

Prevalence and market share should be monitored, particularly in markets targeted by manufacturers.

In line with recommendations for e-cigarette use, measures should go beyond lifetime use or past 30-day use to assess current use; uptake and use should be assessed by smoking status.

Monitoring should include transitions between smoking, e-cigarette use and heated tobacco product use.

Policy

The available evidence suggests that heated tobacco products may be considerably less harmful than tobacco cigarettes and more harmful than e-cigarettes.

With a diverse and mature e-cigarette market in the UK, it is currently not clear whether heated tobacco products provide any advantage as an additional potential harm reduction product.

Depending on emerging evidence on their relative risk compared to combustible tobacco and e-cigarettes, regulatory levers such as taxation and accessibility restrictions should be applied to favour the least harmful options alongside continued efforts to encourage and support complete cessation of tobacco use.

2 March 2018

⇨ The above extract is reprinted with kind permission from Public Health England. Please visit www.gov.uk for further information.

Tobacco company launches foundation to stub out smoking

Philip Morris International say their Foundation for a Smoke-Free World aims to accelerate the end of smoking, but anti-tobacco campaigners are sceptical.

By Sarah Boseley, Health Editor

One of the world's biggest tobacco companies has launched the Foundation for a Smoke-Free World, claiming that it wants to see a future in which people will stop smoking its cigarettes.

Philip Morris International (PMI) says its future is in e-cigarettes and other smoke-free nicotine delivery systems, but anti-tobacco campaigners were highly sceptical, pointing out that it had not stopped marketing the cigarettes it agrees are harmful.

In a public relations coup for PMI, the foundation will be headed by Derek Yach, a former senior figure at the World Health Organization who was responsible for the launch of its global tobacco control treaty.

"I have been working with PMI to establish a foundation to accelerate the end of smoking and tackle the consequences for tobacco farmers," said Yach in an email. "From the start, the intent has been to create an independent foundation that meets the very highest standards of legal and ethical norms and that addresses scientific verification in innovative and needed ways."

But he added: "For many of you this will raise many concerns given my background and PMI's stance on tobacco."

Yach is one of many who believe that vaping offers real possibilities for cutting smoking globally, but others say the tobacco industry has to remain a pariah until such time as it stops promoting lethal cigarettes.

"This should be viewed with the same amount of skepticism as any other announcement from PMI would receive," said Cloe Franko from the campaigning organisation Corporate Accountability International.

"With more and more countries implementing the lifesaving measures of the global tobacco treaty and institutions like the UN Global Compact severing ties, one has to wonder if this is simply another attempt by PMI to regain a lost foothold in international and public health arenas. At the very least, this is clearly an attempt to lock in e-cigarettes and other 'reduced harm' products as the solution to the public health epidemic that PMI continues to drive and profit from.

"Simply put, if Exxon Mobil launched a foundation to combat climate change, would anyone take it seriously?"

Vince Willmore, vice president of communications at the Campaign for Tobacco-Free Kids said: "The company's claimed commitment to a 'smoke-free world' cannot be taken seriously so long as it continues to aggressively market cigarettes and fight proven policies to reduce smoking around the world. Until Philip Morris ceases these harmful activities, its claims should be seen as yet another public relations stunt aimed at repairing the company's image and not a serious effort to reduce the death and disease caused by its products.

"If Philip Morris is truly committed to a smoke-free world, it should immediately take two steps: 1) Actively support the policies to reduce cigarette smoking that are endorsed by the public health community and an international public health treaty, the WHO Framework Convention on Tobacco Control; and 2) set an example for the tobacco industry by stopping all marketing of cigarettes."

ASH (Action on Smoking for Health) said that research funded by the tobacco industry has not been reliable. "The tobacco industry has a terrible track record of funding research designed to support its efforts to block policies to cut smoking. Only recently, Mr Justice Green, who found against the tobacco manufacturers in the UK standard packs court case, concluded that the industry research evidence 'fell significantly below internationally accepted best practice'. PMI may say this time will be different, but it will have to prove it. Tobacco industry claims can never be accepted at face value," said its chief executive Deborah Arnott.

13 September 2017

⇨ The above information is reprinted with kind permission from *The Guardian*. Please visit www.theguardian.com for further information.

Has the UK's anti-smoking efforts reached its peak?

There are still 9.1 million smokers in the UK. Banning, taxation and health education have their limits. Should we take another approach?

By Mark Baker

When is a cigarette company not a cigarette company? When it stops selling cigarettes, and starts selling nicotine. Many people mistakenly view the two as the same thing, they are not. The overwhelming harm from smoking comes from the cocktail of more than 4,000 chemicals released from the combustion of tobacco, many of which are poisonous, and more than 70 of which may cause cancer. While nicotine is an addictive drug, a 2016 Royal College of Physicians (RCP) report found "nicotine alone in the doses used by smokers represents little if any hazard to the user". It is the tobacco smoke not the nicotine that does the damage.

The UK has some of the world's most stringent anti-smoking policies, and the results in getting smokers to stub out the cigarette is something to be proud of – going from 45 per cent of the population who smoked in the 1970s to 15.5 per cent by 2015. However, smoking is still the primary cause of preventable illness and death. The NHS points to 474,000 hospital admissions and 79,000 deaths per year attributable to smoking.

Smokers under the age of 40 have a five times greater risk of a heart attack than non-smokers. Smoking causes about 80 per cent of deaths from lung cancer, around 80 per cent of deaths from bronchitis and emphysema, and about 14 per cent of deaths from heart disease. More than one quarter of all cancer deaths can be attributed to smoking. Smoking causes stroke, diabetes and chronic obstructive pulmonary disease. About half of all life-long smokers will die prematurely. On average, cigarette smokers die ten years younger than non-smokers.

Have government policies, taxation and health campaigns, designed to encourage smokers to give up reached their peak? Despite tremendous gains the rate of smokers quitting has slowed in recent years. The vast majority of smokers know that smoking is bad for health but the UK still has 9.1 million adult smokers.

Giving people more health information to encourage them to make better health choices has limits in effectiveness. Taxation and banning from the public sphere also has its limits. There is still a sizeable portion of the population who continue to smoke, regardless of regulation or public education campaigns – it is unreasonable and naive to assume that policy can make everyone quit smoking. Many don't want to stop; some do, but can't.

Worldwide there are one billion smokers. Tobacco use causes nearly seven million deaths per year. This is a global challenge, so it's necessary to be pragmatic and come up with fresh ideas. 'Reduction of harm' is the second wave of combatting the scourge of tobacco. This may mean having to have uncomfortable 'alliances' as a means to an end, with improved health outcomes for hundreds of millions as the prize.

In recent years there has been a breakthrough in technology where nicotine, which doesn't kill, can be delivered separately from the tar and chemicals, which do. Electronic cigarettes (e-cigarettes) or "vapourisers" were first released to the market in about 2007, they are handheld battery-operated devices that deliver nicotine-containing vapour. They generally consist of a cartridge containing liquid nicotine (eliquid) of varying concentrations, an atomiser and heating device, and a mouthpiece. E-cigarettes contain no tobacco. The year 2012 saw the first involvement of the tobacco industry in the sales of vapour products. Since then, all the Big Tobacco companies have introduced e-cigarettes of their own, now accounting for about half of the global vapour products market.

The charity, Action on Smoking and Health (ASH) estimate that 2.9 million adults in the UK use e-cigarettes, up from 700,000 in 2012. More than half (52 per cent) e-cigarette users are ex-smokers and 45 per cent are still smokers. The main reason given by ex-smokers who are currently vaping is to help them stop smoking, while for current smokers the main reason is to reduce the amount they smoke. ASH advise, "that potential health benefits of e-cigarettes as a means of helping smokers to cut down and quit smoking are significant. Therefore, it is not only appropriate, but indeed essential for health campaigns and local stop-smoking services to develop messaging helping people make the switch from tobacco to e-cigarette use, including by making reference to the devices themselves and providing factual information about them."

Public Health England (PHE) confirm that e-cigarettes are 95 per cent less harmful to health than normal cigarettes, and when supported by a smoking cessation service, help most smokers to quit tobacco altogether. This is endorsed by Cancer Research UK and the British Medical Association. In reference to a 2016 report by the RCP, Professor John Britton, chair of the RCP's Tobacco Advisory Group, stated: "This report lays to rest almost all of the concerns over these products, and concludes that, with sensible regulation, electronic cigarettes have the potential to make a major contribution towards preventing the premature death, disease and social inequalities in health that smoking currently causes in the UK. Smokers should be reassured that these products can help them quit all tobacco use forever."

The harm reduction approach works, but it needs to go further. ASH believes the numbers of smokers who are swapping to e-cigarettes is slowing, and that not enough smokers are aware that vaping is less harmful than smoking. There is a need for clear and balanced information on the relative harm of e-cigarettes and cigarettes. Is it time to allow limited advertising or information awareness to help smokers make the switch?

Many organisations and individuals who have over the years campaigned fiercely against Big Tobacco are against the idea of 'promoting' e-cigarettes for it seems, two reasons: firstly, they conflate vaping with smoking. Secondly, they don't trust Big Tobacco and regard their conversion to e-cigarettes as a cynical attempt at PR.

The first reason is incorrect – vaping is not smoking tobacco. The second reason is not unjustified considering the deceitful history of the cigarette industry.

In a seemingly remarkable shift, Philip Morris International (PMI) the cigarette and tobacco manufacturing company, and owners of the Marlboro brand, has announced its intention to transition its resources from cigarettes to smoke-free alternatives, and to switch its adult smokers to these alternatives as quickly as possible around the world. Is it possible that a cigarette company intends to stop selling cigarettes? Sceptics argue that this is a ploy by PMI to expand its vaping market while still retaining its global cigarette market. Is it? Has PMI developed a conscience? Or does it realise that it's no longer sustainable to base its profits on such a vilified product? The future for tobacco is not going to get any easier. Countries and markets that have less regulation than the UK will likely get tougher. Perhaps PMI is being pragmatic in its drive to deliver nicotine without the harm of tobacco combustion? If it really is transitioning away from cigarettes this is a major positive development regardless of the reasons.

In order to help people understand the benefits of harm reduction, further

evidence-based research is needed, but there is a void in the research due to a lack of funding. This is where the Foundation for a Smoke-Free World may have a significant role to play. Set up in September last year, the foundation's goals are to accelerate global efforts to reduce health impacts and deaths from smoking, with the ultimate goal of eliminating smoking worldwide. It argues that knowledge gaps are impeding progress in research – more needs to be done to assess the effectiveness of the approaches to smoking harm reduction. The Foundation has the money to make a huge impact in this area, but this is where it comes under criticism – it is receiving funding of $80 million (£56 million) a year for the next 12 years, from PMI.

Smoke-Free World is headed by Dr Derek Yach, formerly a director of the World Health Organization (WHO).

According to the Foundation, "the grant terms, bylaws and non-profit status of the Foundation preclude PMI or other tobacco industry representatives from involvement in Foundation governance, or from having any influence over the Foundation's funding decisions, strategy or activities."

The cynics and sceptics are obviously having a field day, but are they letting their dogma get in the way of progress? During his tenure at WHO, Yach served as cabinet director under director-general Gro Harlem Brundtland, where he led the development of WHO's Framework Convention on Tobacco Control and the Global Strategy on Diet and Physical Activity. Yach has been a passionate health advocate and campaigner for many years, he argues that to progress it is necessary to consider all approaches. Over 12 years the Foundation will have almost $1 billion to contribute to the advancement of smoking cessation and reduction of harm. If Smoke-Free World proves to be independent and transparent in its activities and research recommendations, it sounds like an opportunity too important to be missed because of entrenched dogma.

Smokers need help and information to encourage them to transition to a product that does 95 per cent less harm. More research needs to be done to assess the long-term safety of e-cigarettes and related products, to ensure that one type of harm isn't simply being replaced by another type of harm. However, research so far is encouraging. Some smokers want to give up; the UK's major health bodies agree that e-cigarettes are proven to be more effective at helping smokers quit tobacco than other smoking cessation aids. We should acknowledge that many smokers don't want to give up. As part of a proactive campaign encouraging this cohort to transition to vaping products, we should make a regulatory distinction between e-cigarettes and cigarettes, so that further strides can be made in reducing those 79,000 deaths every year in the UK. Globally, the health of one billion lives is at stake.

6 February 2018

⇨ The above information is reprinted with kind permission from *The Independent*. Please visit www.independent.co.uk for further information.

Hospital smoking ban forces patients onto dangerous roads, says trust

By Henry Bodkin

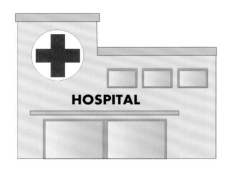

An NHS hospital is refusing to ban smoking on its premises because it believes doing so would put patients in danger of speeding vehicles.

The bosses of Royal Bournemouth and Christchurch Hospitals in Dorset are defending their use of designated smoking areas despite pressure from government health officials.

The trust said it had previously tried a ban of smoking on its grounds, but that this had only forced smokers dangerously close to the adjacent main road where cars and lorries frequently travel at 50 mph.

Last week, Public Health England chief executive Duncan Selbie wrote to all NHS trusts urging them to impose total bans on their premises, despite the fact around one-quarter of patients smoke.

Royal Bournemouth's stance has provoked criticism from anti-smoking groups, who have pointed out that tobacco causes 50 times more deaths each year than road accidents.

But the trust's chief operating officer, Richard Renaut, said: "We currently have a number of designated smoking areas across the Trust.

"If we ban smoking on our grounds altogether, as we have tried, it pushes staff, patients and visitors to smoke close to the main roads around the hospital, which compromises their personal safety, especially at night."

Nearby Poole hospital is also allowing smokers to continue lighting up on their premises in designated shelters "away from the main hospital buildings".

The National Institute for Health and Care Excellence, which sets guidance for clinical practice, states that hospital premises, including the grounds, should remain smoke free.

An article in the *British Medical Journal* last month argued that allowing patients to smoke was a form of "collusion" and "misguided sympathy" on the part of hospital staff.

Deborah Arnott, chief executive of the campaign group ASH, said: "Smoking is still the leading cause of preventable premature death in Britain killing nearly 100,000 people a year compared to less than 2,000 who die from road traffic accidents.

"The single most important change that smokers can make to improve their health is quit – Bournemouth should be doing more to support quitting not facilitating smoking."

Mr Renaut said his trust took proactive measures to persuade smokers to give up their habit.

3 March 2017

⇨ The above information is reprinted with kind permission from *The Telegraph*. Please visit www.telegraph.co.uk for further information.

This group of people have benefitted most from the UK smoking ban

And it isn't smokers...

By Sophie Gallagher

A decade since the UK public smoking ban was introduced, researchers have been finding out who has benefitted most from the changes.

And the new study from Lancaster University has found there is one group whose well-being has improved more than all other demographics – married women with children.

This finding is particularly important because it highlights the welfare impact extends beyond just smokers themselves.

The World Health Organization reports that every single year seven million deaths worldwide are directly caused by the habit, which leads to diseases such as cancer, heart disease and strokes.

They also say that tobacco kills 50% of its users.

Ten years ago it was hoped that the ban, which stopped smokers from lighting up in enclosed spaces (such as pubs and restaurants) from 2006 in Scotland and 2007 in England, would motivate people to quit.

And to mitigate some of the negative effects of second-hand smoke on nonsmokers sharing those communal areas.

But, what the scientists (and government) at the time could not predict, was who would feel the greatest change in their well-being levels as a result.

Now the scientists have analysed data from the British Household Panel Survey, where participants (who were a mix of regular smokers, occasional smokers and complete non-smokers) self-reported psychological well-being before and after the introduction of the ban.

They found married women with children reported the largest increase in well-being but there was no comparable increase for married men with children.

There were also increases in happiness among married men who quit after the ban, and married men and women who never smoked (regardless of whether their partner did).

Dr Eugenio Zucchelli, said: "We find that public smoking bans appear to have a statistically significant short-term positive impact on the well-being of married individuals, especially among women with dependent children."

And Zucchelli speculates that the reason for this increased well-being in this group is "altruistic preference towards their children" that benefits from their decreased concern about second-hand smoke exposure.

Although this is positive news, reports have suggested that the Government could do more good by further taxing cigarettes.

Global studies have found that increasing taxes on cigarettes to 75% of their price in 14 regions had a bigger impact than smoking bans.

Tax rises prevented 3.5 million smoking-related deaths while 'smoke-free air laws' averted 2.5 million deaths.

5 December 2015

⇨ The above information is reprinted with kind permission from The Huffington Post UK. Please visit www.huffingtonpost.co.uk for further information.

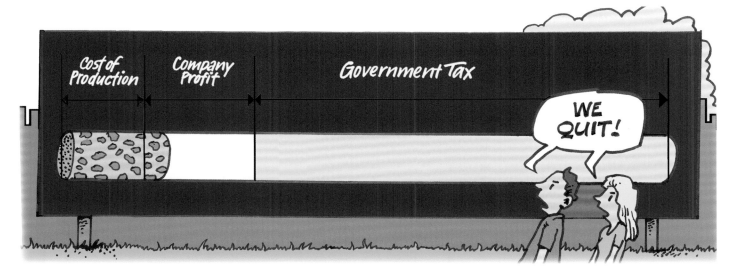

Anti-smoking TV advert shows damaging effects of poisons from cigarette tar

One person is admitted to hospital every minute due to smoking.

A hard-hitting new TV advert shows how poisons from the tar in cigarettes enter the bloodstream and flow through the body within seconds, causing damage to major organs.

The campaign also highlights how smoking can lead to elevated levels of cadmium – a metal used in batteries – in the blood, as well as cancer-causing nitrosamines and carbon monoxide.

Public Health England (PHE) has released the advert to urge the country's seven million smokers to have a go at quitting this New Year.

PHE director of health improvement, Professor John Newton said people know that tar damages the lungs, but it is less well understood that the poisons also reach the other major organs in the body.

"Our new TV ad shows how every cigarette sends a flood of poisonous chemicals through the bloodstream in seconds," Professor Newton said. "We are urging every smoker to take advantage of the free Smokefree support and quit for good this New Year."

TV presenter and entrepreneur Hilary Devey, a former investor on *Dragon's Den*, appears in a film to support the new advert, and vows to give up her 40-year habit after taking part in tests and seeing all the toxic substances in her blood.

The 60-year-old describes how she has smoked from the age of around 14, apart from a break of a few years when she had her son and said even suffering a stroke three years ago only led to her stopping temporarily.

"I've smoked at least 20 a day for over 40 years," she said. "Like many, I've been hooked on cigarettes and ignoring the damage – even though I know the harm I'm doing.

"I've found it extremely difficult to quit for good. Seeing the high levels of poisonous chemicals in my blood from these tests really hit home how dangerous continuing to smoke is – and for that reason, I'm done."

Every year, smoking kills 79,000 people in England, while for every death, another 20 smokers have a smoking-related disease, he said. One person is admitted to hospital every minute due to smoking.

More than 4,000 chemicals are released into the body with each cigarette, including more than 70 known cancer-causing compounds. Exposure to cadmium for a long period of time is associated with an increased risk of damage to the kidneys and bones and may lead to lung cancer.

Research has shown that those who smoke 20 or more cigarettes a day are twice as likely to develop kidney cancer as a non-smoker. Other cancers

associated with smoking include cancers of the pancreas, mouth, respiratory and digestive tracts.

Meanwhile carbon monoxide decreases the ability of the blood to carry oxygen, putting a strain on the heart. It is also associated with an increased risk of blood clots and coronary heart disease.

PHE said there are many ways to quit, including free proven support from NHS Smokefree. Face-to-face help, stop smoking aids, a quitting app, email, social media, and SMS support are all available for people to try and find out what suits them.

Health minister Steve Brine added: "Smoking kills tens of thousands of people every year and a long-term smoker loses an average of ten years of their life. Although smoking rates are at their lowest level in decades, seven million of us still haven't kicked the habit.

"When people see the devastating impact on their health and lives, I hope they will make a change to protect themselves and their families."

29 December 2017

⇨ The above information is reprinted with kind permission from The Huffington Post UK. Please visit www.huffingtonpost.co.uk for further information.

© 2018 Oath (UK) Limited

Stop smoking

Stop smoking and reap the financial and health benefits for years to come, as our three ex-smokers have found.

How quitting gave Allen more time with his family

Before he quit smoking, Allen Champion, 53, from Cambridge, was doing two part-time jobs as a taxi driver and a bus driver, on top of his full-time role as a Park and Ride site coordinator, just to sustain his 50-a-day addiction.

Allen has now packed in smoking, and given up both of his extra jobs, giving him more family time.

"My daughter Roxanne was delighted when I quit," says Allen. "Even from an early age, she'd complained about my smoking." Roxanne was over the moon when, on 26 December 2009, Allen reached a year of not smoking, and now the day serves as an annual reminder of his achievement. "She has a big grin on her face every Boxing Day," he says.

Allen now classes himself as a non-smoker. "It's made a huge difference to my life," he says. "I don't have to work 14- to 16-hour days, six days a week, which means I have more time to spend with my family. That's more precious to me than money."

If Allen hadn't quit smoking just over four years ago, he would have needed to earn £27,147 just to carry on funding his smoking addiction up until now. That's a lot of extra miles he would have had to clock up on his taxi meter.

How Andreena and Stefan quit for their kids' sake

Andreena Bogle-Walton, 31, from Walthamstow in London, says she has more money since quitting her 15-a-day habit, some of which she spends on enjoying extra time with her daughter, Renée.

"I was always broke when I smoked. Now I have more money to take Renée out," says Andreena. "We go to the cinema, we go out to eat and I'm able to buy her more clothes and books as she really enjoys reading. Plus, if Renée comes to me asking for help with her homework, we'll sit down together. I no longer tell her to go to her room because I'm smoking. That's gone now."

Andreena decided to pack in cigarettes when Renée, who was seven at the time, came home from school having learnt about the risks. "She said, 'Mummy, you're going to die.' She just wouldn't let it go. I did it for her," Andreena says.

Similarly, Stefan Klincewicz, 41, resolved to quit when prompted by his eldest daughter, Eva, when she was seven years old. "She would ask me why I was smoking and say I was going to die. Her asking me to stop made me take action – I did it for her sake," he says.

How Stefan turned from a smoker into a marathon runner

Stefan joined an NHS Stop Smoking Service for support, where he says he learnt "a few golden nuggets" about how to use patches and gum properly.

He also started running to take his mind off his cravings. Soon he was enjoying it, running longer distances and even competing in 5km races at his local park in Guildford. He became a regular and someone suggested that he join a running club.

In April 2011, he ran the London Marathon. It was the first of 15 marathons, and he is about to take part in the gruelling Marathon des Sables – a six-day, 151-mile race, which will take him across the Sahara desert.

"I have never felt as well as I do now," says Stefan. "I feel razor-sharp, full of energy, more positive, more alive."

In Andreena's case, quitting smoking was a career-changing decision. After being smoke-free for five months, she resigned from her job as a hospital administrator to retrain as an NHS stop smoking adviser. "I felt if I could take on smoking and conquer it, I could do anything," she says. She is now a specialist stop smoking adviser for City and Hackney.

Not everyone who stops smoking will run a marathon or change their career, but giving up is still the single best thing you can do for your health. After just 20 minutes, your blood pressure and pulse return to normal and, after 24 hours, the carbon monoxide is eliminated from your body.

Quitting also reduces your risk of dying from coronary heart disease. One year after giving up, your risk of dying from coronary heart disease is halved and, after 15 years, your risk falls to the same level as someone who has never smoked cigarettes.

Help with giving up

Still, quitting isn't easy.

"Every smoker knows the dangers, but until it really affects them, there's just no real reason to quit," says Andreena. "I know what it's like to have one cigarette left and not be able to smoke it at night because you know you'll need it in the morning."

Andreena used a combination of patches and gum to help her quit and was supported by a stop smoking adviser who helped to keep her on track whenever she felt tempted.

Quitting was hard for Allen, too. "My father and his brothers were all smokers and died through heart-related diseases," says Allen. "Over the years, I've tried every possible method of quitting." The breakthrough came when his GP recommended he try the drug Champix, which reduces the cravings and helps with nicotine withdrawal symptoms. The medication helped Allen quit successfully.

⇨ The above information is reprinted with kind permission from The British Heart Foundation. Please visit www.bhf.org.uk for further information.

© British Heart Foundation

Ten years of the smoking ban – what's changed in Wales?

Sunday 2 April marks ten years since the ground-breaking legislation banning smoking in enclosed public places came into force across Wales.

The hotly debated ban has helped to drastically bring down smoking rates among adults and teenagers alike and saved thousands from the harms of a product which kills one in two of its long-term users.

In 2007, 24% of adults in Wales smoked, now levels stand at 19% – over 94,000 less smokers. The stats are even greater when it comes to teens, with smoking rates reduced by 6% for boys and 14% for girls, respectively.

A major cultural shift has taken place over the past decade. A vast decrease in the numbers of those who smoke in the home, from 80% to 46% since the ban's implementation, suggests a better awareness of the dangers of second-hand smoke, especially around children and families.

Chief executive of tobacco control campaign charity ASH Wales, Suzanne Cass, said: "The smoking ban has resulted in the most positive improvement in the nation's health in decades. The significance of this legislation should not be underestimated. Thousands more children now live in a smokefree home, and hundreds of thousands of people are no longer subjected to the deadly effects of passive smoking."

There is clear evidence smokers no longer feel as comfortable smoking around others – the number of people smoking in their own home has almost halved since the ban came into place. It is fantastic to see the message about the dangers of smoking, especially around children, is being heard."

The hidden threat from second-hand smoke, especially for workers in the leisure industry such as pubs and clubs, was cited as one of the major reasons for bringing in the indoor smoking ban. The World Health Organization says more than 80% of cigarette smoke is invisible and odourless, and there is no safe level of second-hand smoke exposure.

There continues to be strong support for the smoking ban in Wales, with 81% of people in support of the smokefree legislation. Notably three-quarters of smokers are in favour of the ban.

2007 – SMOKING BANNED INDOORS AND IN SUBSTANTIALLY ENCLOSED PLACES

2012 – CIGARETTES HIDDEN FROM VIEW IN ALL LARGE SUPERMARKETS

2015 – SMOKING BANNED IN CARS WHEN SOMEONE UNDER 18 IS PRESENT

2016 – TWO WELSH BEAUTY SPOTS BECOME VOLUNTARILY SMOKFREE

2016 – PLAIN PACKAGING STARTS TO APPEAR IN SHOPS

2017 – EVERY PLAYGROUND IN WALES BECOMES VOLUNTARILY SMOKEFREE

2017 – WELSH GOVERNMENT PLANS TO LEGISLATE AGAINST SMOKING AT HOSPITALS, PLAYGROUNDS AND SCHOOLS

Despite the huge steps forward, ASH Wales believes there are still more changes to be had. Suzanne continued; "Smoking rates have dropped for most of the population except among the unemployed where they've in fact increased from 41% to 43%. This shows the stop smoking message still isn't engaging these 'hard-to-reach' people and the health inequalities gap between the 'haves' and the 'have nots' in Wales is increasing."

Substantial laws and voluntary bans have come into force in Wales over the past decade since the implementation of the smokefree legislation…

2007

⇨ 24% of people smoke in Wales

⇨ The age limit to buy tobacco is raised to 18 from 16

2012

⇨ Cigarettes must be hidden from view in all large supermarkets

⇨ Cigarette vending machines are banned in Wales

2015

⇨ It becomes illegal to smoke in a car when a young person is present

⇨ The sale of e-cigarettes to under-18s is banned

2016

⇨ The first beaches in Wales, Caswell Bay and Little Haven, become smokefree

⇨ All cigarettes made from 2016 must be in drab, green-brown 'plain' packaging

⇨ Every children's playground in Wales became voluntarily smokefree zones

2017

⇨ 19% of people smoke in Wales

⇨ Welsh Government plans to legislate against smoking on hospital grounds, school grounds and at children's playgrounds

⇨ 11 Welsh local authorities voluntarily make their primary school gates 'no smoking' areas

⇨ Packs of ten are no longer on sale.

1 April 2017

⇨ The above information is reprinted with kind permission from ASH Wales Cymru. Please visit www.ashwales.org.uk for further information.

Key facts

- Smoking is by far the greatest avoidable risk for developing many types of cancer. (page 1)

- Smoking damages your blood vessels and increases your risk of getting heart disease and of having a stroke. (page 1)

- Cigarette smoke contains at least 4,000 chemical compounds and of these, more than 40 are known to cause cancer. (page 1)

- Men who smoke are likely to have fewer sperm. The sperm are also more likely to be damaged so they are less able to fertilise an egg. You're also at a greater risk of erectile dysfunction if you smoke. (page 1)

- If you smoke 20 or more cigarettes a day, your risk of having a stroke can be up to six times that of a non-smoker. (page 1)

- Smoking can prematurely age you by ten years or more, and you're more likely to get wrinkles on your face at a younger age. (page 1)

- Tobacco kills more than seven million people each year. More than six million of those deaths are the result of direct tobacco use while around 890,000 are the result of non-smokers being exposed to second-hand smoke. (page 2)

- In adults, second-hand smoke causes serious cardiovascular and respiratory diseases, including coronary heart disease and lung cancer. In infants, it causes sudden death. In pregnant women, it causes low birth weight. (page 2)

- Almost half of children regularly breathe air polluted by tobacco smoke in public places (page 2)

- Second-hand smoke causes more than 890,000 premature deaths per year. (page 2)

- In 2004, children accounted for 28% of the deaths attributable to second-hand smoke. (page 2)

- Around 44% of the world's population live in the 43 countries that have aired at least one strong anti-tobacco mass media campaign within the last two years. (page 3)

- Scientists from the University of Bristol have looked at all 14,500 participants in 'Children of the 90s' and found that if a girl's maternal grandmother smoked during pregnancy, the girl is 67 per cent more likely to display certain traits linked to autism, such as poor social communication skills and repetitive behaviours. (page 6)

- 55% of children aged 14 and 15 who smoke say they buy illegal tobacco from sources like 'tab houses' and shops – while 73% say they have been offered illegal tobacco. (page 7)

- Each year about 600,000 people die from exposure to second-hand tobacco smoke (inhaling other people's cigarette smoke). (page 8)

- e-cigarettes could be contributing to at least 20,000 successful new quits per year and possibly many more. (page 10)

- many thousands of smokers incorrectly believe that vaping is as harmful as smoking; around 40% of smokers have not even tried an e-cigarette. (page 10)

- Since October last year, anyone caught smoking in a vehicle carrying someone under the age of 18 has been breaking the law and could face a £50 fine. (page 14)

- Experts think up to three million children are exposed to smoke in cars, putting them at risk of serious conditions including asthma, bronchitis and infections of the chest and ear. (page 14)

- Cardiovascular disease, not cancer, is the greatest mortality risk for smoking, causing about 48% of smoking-related premature deaths. (page 16)

- Every year around 100,000 people in the UK die from smoking, with many more living with debilitating smoking-related illnesses. (page 19)

- Smoking causes about 90% of lung cancers. (page 19)

- Smokers are also more likely than non-smokers to develop depression or anxiety disorder over time. (page 22)

- The overwhelming harm from smoking comes from the cocktail of more than 4,000 chemicals released from the combustion of tobacco, many of which are poisonous, and more than 70 of which may cause cancer. (page 32)

- Worldwide there are one billion smokers. (page 32)

- Smoking is still the leading cause of preventable premature death in Britain killing nearly 100,000 people a year compared to less than 2,000 who die from road traffic accidents. (page 34)

- Global studies have found that increasing taxes on cigarettes to 75% of their price in 14 regions had a bigger impact than smoking bans. (page 35)

- Research has shown that those who smoke 20 or more cigarettes a day are twice as likely to develop kidney cancer as a non-smoker. Other cancers associated with smoking include cancers of the pancreas, mouth, respiratory and digestive tracts. (page 36)

- Carbon monoxide decreases the ability of the blood to carry oxygen, putting a strain on the heart. It is also associated with an increased risk of blood clots and coronary heart disease. (page 37)

Accetone

Widely used as a solvent, for example in nail polish remover, acetone is one of around 4,000 chemicals contained in the average cigarette.

Ammonia

A chemical found in cleaning fluids, ammonia is inhaled during smoking.

Cadmium

A metal used in batteries, also contained in tobacco.

Cigarette

A paper tube filled with tobacco which is lit at one end and inhaled orally (smoked). There are many slang words for cigarettes, including fags, tabs, smokes and cigs/ciggies. Cigarettes can be bought pre-prepared or hand-rolled. Most modern cigarettes contain a spongy filter which reduces the amount of poisonous chemicals inhaled while smoking: however, a large part of these substances are still absorbed and smoking therefore poses a substantial health risk.

Cyanide

A poisonous compound, found in tobacco smoke.

E-cigarette

A battery-operated device that is typically designed to resemble a traditional cigarette and is used to inhale a usually nicotine-containing vapour

Formaldehyde

A chemical used to preserve corpses. Formaldehyde is contained in tobacco.

Nicotine

An addictive chemical compound found in the nightshade family of plants that makes up about 0.6–3.0% of dry weight of tobacco. It is the nicotine contained in tobacco which causes smokers to become addicted, and many will use Nicotine Replacement Therapy such as patches, gum or electronic cigarettes to help them deal with cravings while quitting.

Passive smoking

Passive smoking refers to the inhalation of tobacco smoke by someone other than the smoker: for example, a parent smoking near their children may expose them to the poisonous chemicals in the second-hand smoke from their cigarette. This has been shown to have a negative impact on the passive smoker's health.

Smoking ban

The prohibition of smoking cigarettes, etc. in public places

Tobacco

Tobacco is a brown herb-like substance produced from the dried leaves of tobacco plants. The tobacco used in cigarettes contains many substances dangerous to the user when inhaled, including tar, which can cause lung cancer, and nicotine, which is highly addictive. Nevertheless, around 21 per cent of adults in the UK are smokers.

Tobacco duty

An abbreviation of tobacco products duty, it is a type of tax charged on purchases of tobacco products.

Assignments

Brainstorming

⇨ In small groups discuss what you know about smoking

⇨ List as many brands of cigarettes you can think of

⇨ What is second-hand smoke?

Research

⇨ Conduct a survey amongst your classmates and parents. How many of them smoke? What is the ratio of men against women amongst them who smoke? What are the age groups affected? You should ask at least eight questions and produce a graph to show your findings.

⇨ Do some research into COPD. What does this term stand for? What are the health implications of contracting this disease? Write a short report on your findings.

⇨ In pairs, do some research into e-cigarettes. Find out how they affect your health in comparison with normal cigarettes. Produce a pie chart to show your findings.

⇨ Research the different products which are available to help you give up smoking. Write a report listing as many as you can and the ways in which they can help.

⇨ In small groups, research what impact the smoking ban has had. You should consider the effect it has had on the leisure industry which includes pubs and clubs. Do you agree with the smoking ban? Write a report on your findings and share it with the rest of your class.

⇨ Do some research into the health benefits to a person once they have given up smoking. Make a list of all the benefits you can think of and then produce a chart to show your findings. Share this with your class.

Design

⇨ Imagine you are working for an anti-smoking charity. Produce a poster which could be displayed in public places such as bus stops and tube stations.

⇨ In pairs, design an e-cigarette.

⇨ In groups, produce a leaflet informing people about the risks of smoking and the benefits to be gained from giving up. It should also inform them of the different anti-smoking devices which are available.

⇨ Imagine you work for a company that manufactures e-cigarettes. Your company has released a new e-cigarette, aimed at young people, and wants to try to sell it to teenagers. Write an advert which they might use to advertise this new product. Think about the name of the product and the flavours which might be available.

⇨ Read the article 'Hospital smoking ban forces patients onto dangerous roads'. Design a smoking shelter to be used in the grounds of a hospital.

Oral

⇨ As a class, discuss why you think some young people are using e-cigarettes even though they have never been smokers. Do you think this will lead them to take up smoking cigarettes? What could be done to discourage them from smoking e-cigarettes?

⇨ The article on page 24 says "NHS hospitals should sell e-cigarettes". In small groups, discuss this and give your views on whether you think this would be a positive move towards helping people to give up smoking.

⇨ Choose one of the illustrations from the book and consider what message your chosen picture is trying to get across. How does it support, or add to, the points made in the accompanying article? Do you think it is successful?

⇨ In pairs, create a presentation aimed at teenagers explaining the risks of smoking and suggesting ways in which those who do smoke might be helped to give up.

⇨ Do you think it is appropriate to smoke in front of small children? Debate this as a class.

Reading/writing

⇨ Imagine you are an agony aunt/uncle and have received a letter from a child who is worried about their parents smoking habits. They are scared their parents might die as a result of this. Write a suitable reply.

⇨ Write a blog post from either of these two points of view, explaining why you feel the way you do:

• A mother who is not happy with her son smoking and would like him to give up

• A teenager who is fed up with his parents trying to make him give up smoking.

⇨ The article on page 26 says "ASH Wales welcomes new laws protecting children from smoking'" Write a letter to your local council asking them to make local parks and school gates, smoke-free zones. Explain the reasons why you feel this is important.

⇨ Imagine you work for a charity which campaigns to protect children from second-hand smoke. Write a blog-post for your charity's website explaining the issues around second-hand smoke and why you think it is important that children are not exposed to it.

Acknowledgements

The publisher is grateful for permission to reproduce the material in this book. While every care has been taken to trace and acknowledge copyright, the publisher tenders its apology for any accidental infringement or where copyright has proved untraceable. The publisher would be pleased to come to a suitable arrangement in any such case with the rightful owner.

Images

All images courtesy of iStock except page 26: Morguefile, pages 7, 9,12, 13, 16, 19, 27, 31 and 36 Pixabay.

Illustrations

Don Hatcher: pages 18 & 35. Simon Kneebone: pages 11 & 30. Angelo Madrid: pages 5 & 25.

Additional acknowledgements

With thanks to the Independence team: Shelley Baldry, Danielle Lobban, Jackie Staines and Jan Sunderland.

Tina Brand

Cambridge, June 2018